New Library of Pa

Brief Encounters

New Library of Pastoral Care

STILL SMALL VOICE
An Introduction to Counselling
Michael Jacobs

LETTING GO
Caring for the Dying and Bereaved
Peter Speck and Ian Ainsworth-Smith

LIVING ALONE
The Inward Journey to Fellowship
Martin Israel

LEARNING TO CARE
Christian Reflection on
Pastoral Practice
Michael H. Taylor

MAKE OR BREAK
An Introduction to Marriage
Counselling
Jack Dominian

MEANING IN MADNESS
The Pastor and the Mentally Ill
John Foskett

PAID TO CARE?
The Limits of Professionalism in
Pastoral Care
Alastair V. Campbell

SWIFT TO HEAR
Facilitating Skills in Listening
and Responding
Michael Jacobs

BRIEF ENCOUNTERS
Pastoral Ministry through Baptisms,
Weddings and Funerals
Wesley Carr

LOVE THE STRANGER
Ministry in Multi-Faith Areas
Roger Hooker and Christopher Lamb

BEING THERE
Care in Time of Illness
Peter Speck

GOING SOMEWHERE
People with Mental Handicaps and
their Pastoral Care
Sheila Hollins and Margaret Grimer

MADE IN HEAVEN?
Ministry with Those Intending
Marriage
Peter Chambers

FAMILY MATTERS
The Pastoral Care of Personal
Relationships
Sue Walrond-Skinner

HELPING THE HELPERS
Supervision and Pastoral Care
John Foskett and David Lyall

CITY OF GOD?
Pastoral Care in the Inner City
Nicholas Bradbury

CLERGY STRESS
The Hidden Conflicts in Ministry
Mary Anne Coate

HOLDING IN TRUST
The Appraisal of Ministry
Michael Jacobs

LISTEN TO THE VOICE WITHIN
A Jungian Approach to Pastoral Care
Christopher Perry

BEING YOUR AGE
Pastoral Care for Older People
Michael Butler and Ann Orbach

SIN, GUILT, AND FORGIVENESS
The Hidden Dimensions of a
Pastoral Process
Mary Anne Coate

A DICTIONARY OF
PASTORAL CARE
edited by Alastair V. Campbell

NEW·LIBRARY·OF

PASTORAL·CARE

BRIEF ENCOUNTERS

*Pastoral Ministry through
Baptisms, Weddings and Funerals*

Wesley Carr

First published in Great Britain in 1985
Reprinted three times
This revised edition published in 1994
Society for Promoting Christian Knowledge
Holy Trinity Church
Marylebone Road
London NW1 4DU

British Library Cataloguing-in-Publication Data

A catalogue record for this book is available
from the British Library

ISBN 0-281-04784-7

Filmset by Pioneer Associates (Graphic) Ltd
Printed in Great Britain by
The Cromwell Press, Melksham, Wiltshire

To
The Parochial Clergy and Ministers of the
Diocese of Chelmsford, with whom I have
been privileged to work and minister
1974–1984

Contents

Foreword

The *New Library of Pastoral Care* has been planned to meet the needs of those people concerned with pastoral care, whether clergy or lay, who seek to improve their knowledge and skills in this field. Equally, it is hoped that it may prove useful to those secular helpers who may wish to understand the role of the pastor.

Pastoral care in every age has drawn from contemporary secular knowledge to inform its understanding of men and women and their various needs and of the ways in which these needs might be met. Today it is perhaps the secular helping professions of social work, counselling and psychotherapy, and community development which have particular contributions to make to pastors in their work. Such knowledge does not stand still, and pastors would have a struggle to keep up with the endless tide of new developments which pour out from these and other disciplines, and to sort out which ideas and practices might be relevant to their particular pastoral needs. Among present-day ideas, for instance, of particular value might be an understanding of the social context of the pastoral task, the dynamics of the helping relationship, the attitudes and skills as well as factual knowledge which might make for effective pastoral intervention and, perhaps most significant of all, the study of particular cases, whether through verbatim reports of interviews or general case presentation. The discovery of ways of learning from what one is doing is becoming increasingly important.

There is always a danger that a pastor who drinks deeply at the well of a secular discipline may risk losing a distinct pastoral identity and become 'just another' social worker or counsellor. It in no way detracts from the value of these professions to assert that the role and task of the pastor are quite unique among the helping professions and deserve to be clarified and strengthened rather than weakened. The theological commitment of the pastors and the appropriate use of their role will be a recurrent theme of the series. At the same time pastors cannot afford to work in a vacuum. They need to be able to communicate and co-operate with those helpers in other disciplines whose work may overlap, without loss of their own unique status. This in turn will mean being able to communicate with them through some understanding of their concepts and language.

Finally, there is a rich variety of styles and approaches in pastoral work within the various religious traditions. No attempt will be made to secure a uniform approach. The Library will contain the variety, and even perhaps occasional eccentricity, which such a title suggests. Some books will be more specifically theological and others more concerned with particular areas of need or practice. It is hoped that all of them will have a usefulness that will reach right across the boundaries of religious denomination.

DEREK BLOWS

Preface to New Edition

———

The first edition of this book appeared in 1985. Since then there has been much writing on aspects of pastoral ministry. Studies of baptism, marriage and funerals have been produced. Churches have separately and in ecumenical accord studied these subjects. But there still seems to be a space for this book on pastors' shelves. For I have tried to address what happens to ministers in such encounters and the range of expectations, overt and covert, to which they are subjected.

To many it may seem remarkable that people still turn to the church for these offices. Numbers are generally lower. Statistics matter, but they have to be set in context. To what extent, for instance, is the decline in the number of church weddings to do with different attitudes to matrimony on the part of couples or changes in the way that the churches have responded to them? The same can be said of baptisms and funerals. In the Church of England, for instance, hitherto unheard of discussions are now held by some clergy as to whether they should conduct the funeral of a non-attender. Whatever the precise statistics, we do have evidence, both of the persistence of these offices and more generally, that religion is not about to die out. Whether the Christian churches can cope with it is another matter. It is dangerous to prophesy. But we might judge that if people generally are once again becoming slightly more religiously aware, then there is a distinctive opportunity for mission and evangelism on the part of those churches which do not despise or withdraw from the messiness of human life. And baptisms, weddings and funerals provide many such contacts.

Inevitably this writing betrays a perspective that is chiefly drawn from the Church of England. I have tried, however, in this revision to take account of justified criticism over language and too Anglican a set of assumptions. I have also studied much of the literature that has appeared since the original writing. But to incorporate all such insights and refer to them in the notes would have required a new book.

Since 1985 the issue of language has become more acute. In this revision 'clergy' mostly disappear and 'pastor' and 'minister' have become preferred, but not exclusive, terms to describe ordained public ministers. Gender is not so easily solved. Throughout it is frequently necessary to refer to the individual minister. In order to do so gender-specific language has to be used. I have, therefore, sometimes used the masculine pronoun and sometimes the feminine to avoid the cumbersome usage of 'him or her'. In each case the use is inclusive of the other gender.

The ideas and attitudes discussed in this book derive from many sources, most of them unacknowledged. Harold Frankham, Vicar of Luton and later Provost of Southwark, taught me, when I was his curate, the importance of this ministry for the wider aims of a parish church. The clergy of the Diocese of Chelmsford are still those to whom I happily dedicate the book. Now I would, however, add the many groups of ministers, lay and ordained, throughout the United Kingdom and Ireland who have stimulated my thinking in response to lectures and courses. Michael Fox (now Archdeacon of Harlow), Timothy Stevens (now Archdeacon of West Ham) and Peter Marshall (now Canon Residentiary of Ripon Cathedral) all helped in 1985 and have done so ever since. Natalie, my wife, knows when to stay out of my way and when to be on hand with support and willingness to take on the drudgery of proof reading. All have stimulated reflection, provided evidence and offered ideas. The inadequacies and inaccuracies, of course, are mine.

One person on reading the first draft commented that it made the job of the minister seem demanding, responsible and important. It is, and remains so even in changed times. If this small work enables my fellow pastors to a better grasp of their role and clarity about their theology and ministry, I shall be honoured.

Wesley Carr
June 1993
Bristol Cathedral

ONE

Introduction: The Occasional Offices

The rites which are used as occasion demands—the occasional offices—are to many people more familiar than those which comprise the regular worship of the church. In the Book of Common Prayer, for example, eight such offices are provided: Baptism, Confirmation, Matrimony, the Visitation of the Sick, the Communion of the Sick, Burial, the Churching of Women, and the Commination. Today, however, for practical purposes in most churches the issues of ministry through these occasional offices arise in connection with the baptism of infants, weddings and funerals. When we begin to think about these, ritual, religion and rites become entangled. Theology, psychology, sociology and anthropology vie for attention, so that we feel overwhelmed by

> Greek endings, each the little passing-bell
> That signifies some faith's about to die.[1]

For all this, the local church and minister experience demands being made which, however they are interpreted and from whatever perspective they are explained, still have to be dealt with. Explanation is not necessarily the means to salvation; neither is confusion. We may, therefore, on the one hand acknowledge the sense of confusion that may be generated in us when our attention is directed to the theory and practice of pastoring. But on the other hand we may also recognize that merely to continue to act without trying to understand is irresponsible. We need to find a means of living in and contributing to the richly problematic area of human life which the church encounters through these occasional offices, without surrendering to the reductionism implicit in some social scientific interpretation or theological approaches. 'Septic human relationships cannot survive in an antiseptic bath of psycho-social formaldehyde.'[2] Ministers, therefore, need to seek a model of pastoral ministry by which to chart their way through the seas of interpretation now available to them and through the waves of demands which strike the local minister in his parish or church.

This book is one of a series on pastoral care and practice. It is not intended as a contribution to the wealth of technical literature on rites, rituals or social customs. Nor is it particularly concerned with the theology of the sacraments. But neither topic can be omitted. Indeed, one of the continuing themes of this essay is the way in which content and context may be too quickly separated in order to escape problems which have to be faced for effective ministry. If a problem is avoided, the chances are that an opportunity will also be missed. Context and content interact. For example, at different moments in their lives a couple may say to each other, 'I love you'. The words are identical, whether they are those of nervous first love, the ardently newly-wed, the unsettling period of mid-life crisis, or of contented old age. But the content of the words changes according to which of these contexts applies. But the context, too, is altered by the fact of the words being uttered. They themselves contribute to the relationship and thus make their own utterance more or less possible. In the present study we shall address this interaction of theology and practice, or of word and context. This may mean that at times major issues may appear to be left aside. But in the course of the total argument I hope to cover the key issues which arise in connection with the occasional offices, although with the clear recognition that on a subject so sensitive as this, major differences are bound to remain.

The occasional offices are a facet of the church's pastoral ministry. This word 'pastoral' is widely used in contemporary discussion and writing on ministry. It seems so frequently attached to some other word—ministry, care, theology, practice—that it assumes an Alice in Wonderland aspect of seeming to mean everything but ending up meaning nothing. When in 1978 the cardinals met in Rome after the sudden death of Pope John Paul I, pastoral factors loomed large. Having only just chosen one pope for his pastoral gifts, they seemed to think that they should find another. Peter Hebblethwaite describes how the discussions developed. 'Pastoral' began to be applied to any and every aspect of ministry. At first it meant 'coming from a diocese', but gradually those in tribunals, lawyers, members of the Curia, and ultimately all the cardinals were described as 'pastoral'. 'Thus "pastoral" became a broken-backed word.'[3] Another, less exalted, example of how this term may be used as a catch-all is taken from the programme for a county youth camp:

> I would like to thank the camp leader, his village helpers and leaders who have supervised a varied programme of activities and dealt with the pastoral side of the camp.

Many similar examples could be cited to illustrate how 'pastoral' tends to be used to cover every eventuality which is not dealt with under some other heading. One area which is germane to the present discussion is that of pastoral counselling. This phrase seems to allow the notion of counselling to be invested with theological aura and thus incorporated uncritically into the range of Christian ministry. Ministers in their enthusiasm become preoccupied with crises and casualties, to whom they feel that they can now offer a professionally competent pastoral counselling ministry. But ministers who have acquired such training often report that they seem not to meet people. Having acquired the skills of counselling, they discover that people do not come for counsel. For them one of the prevailing fantasies of ministers is confirmed. Just as doctors think they are underpaid, so clergy believe that they are unwanted.

The continuing demand for the occasional offices, which will be explored in detail later, suggests that people may desire the church's ministry (though not necessarily counselling) while the church's ministers find it increasingly difficult to perceive that such encounters are ministry. It may be that counselling skills are being sought to authenticate a pastoral ministry, such as has traditionally been offered, as a substitute for the loss of a theological justification for it. If counselling has been assigned a theological aura, so too, perhaps, theology has similarly been invested with a counselling halo. The apparent ignorance of both gospel and church on the part of those who approach the minister may confirm in the minister some sense of a lost theological framework. Confronted, therefore, with counselling assumptions in himself and theological ignorance in the applicants, the minister may find the occasional offices almost too complicated to bear.[4]

There is additionally a question about the role of the minister which is raised by these encounters. The minister's own understanding of his role may seem far from the belief that people display about it. And the meaning of the gospel for them seems to be different from what he believes it should be. Personal problems compound the stress. Dealing with profound human emotions in a raw state, the minister finds his own self also disturbed. Facing a couple with the meaning of marriage brings his own marriage to mind. Committing a corpse to the ground or to the flames reminds him of his own mortality. And all this in a context where central theological issues suddenly become questioning: Is this what God intends mankind to be? Did Christ really die for this world? Is the Kingdom of God any different from the Church? The occasional offices constitute a draining demand on time, energy and emotion. They raise questions about the theological norms and internally determined customs of the contemporary church. And even in the face of the current secularism in British society, they remain a demand with which, at least for the time being, the Christian churches have to deal.

This book is divided into three parts. First there is a general consideration of the occasional offices from a series of perspectives. This includes reflection on the church and its task in society, with some of the consequences of this for its theology and practice. The second part consists of studies of the three primary offices—infant baptism, weddings and funerals. The discussion here is practical. A final chapter draws together some of the pressures on the minister himself and what these may signify, as well as how they may be used in ministry. The divisions are for convenience, but the argument, as I have suggested already, is to be read as a single whole.

Notes

1. Robert Browning, *Bishop Blougram's Apology.*
2. Aidan Kavanagh, 'Life-cycle events, civic ritual and the Christian', in D. Power and L. Maldonado, eds, *Liturgy and Human Passage, Concilium* 112 (1979), pp. 14ff.
3. Peter Hebblethwaite, *The Year of the Three Popes* (London, Collins, 1978), p. 135.
4. David Martin, *A General Theory of Secularisation* (Oxford, Blackwell, 1978), pp. 278ff.

PART ONE

The Theological and Pastoral Significance of the Occasional Offices

TWO

Brief Encounters

In any encounter with someone or some group around a baptism, wedding or funeral, the minister touches something deep about life but necessarily does so in a brief, temporary and transitory engagement. There are few, if any, churches that could encourage such meetings with people at length and in depth. Time is always at a premium for the minister. But, as will be seen, it is unlikely that the applicants would wish for much more, even if it were available. In the nature of the case with an occasional office the encounter is fleeting. In this chapter we shall examine these brief encounters from the perspective of the minister and of those seeking his or her ministry.

Ministers, unless they deliberately isolate themselves from any engagement with people in the community at an instinctive level, are bound to be thrust into the midst of people's expectations of what they ought to do. They regard themselves as ministers of the gospel, even at times in danger of becoming professional Christians. But when approached for the ministry of an occasional office, they find that their Christian gospel seems of little interest. They are immersed in implicit or folk religion. This topic has been widely discussed.[1] People recognize in themselves experiences which they may feel somehow to be 'religious'. From time to time they seek ritual expression for these feelings and for that purpose regard themselves as members of the church.[2] If they feel rejected at this point they become angry, but—and this is an important facet of the occasional offices—may persist in finding what they want by going to another church, and, if need be, more than one.

Nineteenth-century intellectual confidence in the demise of religion has proved misplaced.[3] Indeed today it sometimes seems that it is now the churches themselves which chiefly believe, and act upon that belief, that religion is finished. Polls are notoriously unreliable, but even if the figures are read at their face value, they show that a large number of people still look to the church for a ministry through the occasional offices.[4] And where such figures are low, there is now the suspicion that the churches by their behaviour may be encouraging them to be so. Of all people ministers should not be fooled into believing in the historical inevitability of the decline of religious expression. They may well at times ask themselves whether their appeals to sociological theories of secularization, the rites of passage, and the like, may not be attempts to explain away or rationalize an uncomfortable part of their ministry.

The heavy demand of the occasional offices—both in the sense of being time-consuming as well as in the way in which it puts pressure upon the minister's Christian motivation and understanding—contrasts pointedly with the apparent unproductiveness of such encounters. Even if in the long term a correlation were discerned between this ministry and church membership, there still seems to be no immediate pay-off. In practice people rarely seem to join the congregation or contribute to funds. There is a discontinuity between the criteria of successful ministry that tend to be used by the church as an institution, with its statistical tables and quotas, and the amount of time and energy devoted to people in this immature state of religious expectation. One defence against this is to rationalize the issue, either in terms of why people do not join or in terms of creating conditions which would make it difficult for them to join, even if they wished. What, then, is the place of such a ministry, with this public 'failure' and the guilt (sometimes anger) that is generated in the minister, as he is caught between his gospel and the ordinary life of people?

On top of these pressures from the church and from within, the minister further encounters the belief that such ministries are engagement with people who are outside the church and that they therefore constitute prime opportunities for mission and evangelism. These two words are currently in vogue, and as such they are traps for the unwary. Every meeting with someone who is not a member of the church is a moment of mission. That claim may be true. But to a sensitive minister the encounter around a baptism, wedding or funeral, scarcely feels like that. For mission is essentially 'going to', addressing people, and therefore an aggressive activity. The missionary is sent to an alien environment in order to bring to it something new. Looked at this way applicants for the occasional office present themselves as the missionary. They seem to bring to, what is for them, an alien world of the church and the vicar a believed reality from everyday life, about which the vicar is supposed to know little and understand less. The tables are turned on him as the applicants set the agenda. Indeed, they come to some extent because over the centuries the church has bid them come, sometimes chased after them to come, and generally provided the normal means for ritual expression of aspects of human life. 'In the realm of the imagination, once something extraordinary is produced, it is never lost. Changes in culture only widen the expressive repertoire of mankind.'[5] In such meetings the minister feels that he is more likely to be used than to be able to use the occasion for some form of evangelism or mission. And when he tries to evangelize, he sometimes finds himself in an odd position: whatever he says, people will probably affirm. But there is little or no engagement with what he conceives as his message. Frustration results. To be able to live with this, a profounder understanding of the nature of Christian ministry is required.

The clue to understanding ministry through the occasional offices will not be found within the church. Although they are church rituals, they are not created by the church alone. Nor do they belong solely to the minister. He or she is not the arbiter of what happens. For baptisms, weddings and funerals the church and its ministers need people to approach them. Ministers and churches need to grasp, therefore, that every occasional office is a specific moment of that general connection between the church and its environment.[6] In this context both church and environment are human notions: the church becomes the minister, lay or ordained; the environment is the expectation, hope and maybe fear of those who come for their service. People are remarkably persistent, even in the face of attempts to discourage them. They may be willing to meet every demand that a church may make, such as regular attendance, a training course or the like. If they find one church unhelpful, they may well go to another. And even those who give up, sometimes comment at some later point in their life on their disappointment at having not been able to have the baptism or wedding. Funerals are, as we shall see, still different. Unless this process is appreciated as having some validity in itself, a downward spiral in the relationship between the minister and the applicants ensues. If she is thinking in terms of an opportunity to proclaim the full content of the Christian gospel, she will find an increasing sense that her words and interpretations are neither being heard nor resisted. The resulting sense of guilt at having failed to preach the gospel becomes compounded with a vague feeling of having let God down. This sensation is complicated. For it is sometimes in the act of standing up for the seriousness of the gospel and the awesomeness of God that the minister feels this failure. The result is usually some sort of anger. This may be expressed about the people who came demanding 'their' service. This is frequently voiced in gatherings of ministers as horror stories are shared. Sometimes it is turned on the people themselves, even if the minister believes that he is doing this in a clear but pastoral fashion. They in turn feel rejected and may complain to the bishop or other senior minister. They may even write to the press. It is some evidence about the place of the church in society that the papers are quite likely to report the incident. Perhaps more often than either of these ministers become angry with God for putting them in this position or with themselves for allowing themselves to be there. Anger which is self-directed tends to produce apathy. Ministers, therefore, who cannot grasp what is happening to them in this requested ministry are likely to find their behaviour here affects all other dimensions of their ministry more profoundly than they may realize.

When the structures of the church and social life change, there is a tendency to replace what we might describe as a 'natural' ministerial function with a professional one. The minister, feeling that he is deprived of his distinctive, and to him familiar, role, may seek personal affirmation by acquiring new skills. These tend to be found in the modern human sciences. Through using these he may discover that his own feelings may not be produced merely by his personal emotional state. He may become aware of other factors in people and of the way in which he functions in the larger networks of human relationships. By appreciating these experiences he may, so the argument runs, become a better minister. There is truth in this, and many courses are currently offered to assist ministers to develop and use such understanding. There is also little doubt that contemporary approaches to pastoral care through counselling theory and skills can and do serve the church's ministry. Yet care is needed, not least when the minister is involved with people through the occasional offices, lest superficial connections are made between counselling ideas and Christian ministry. This is especially easy in view of the way that Christian themes and illustrations are widely employed in psychotherapeutically oriented writing and of the apparent correspondence of ideas between applied theology and counselling. The seminal work, for example, of Truax and Carkhuff directs attention away from techniques towards empathy, openness and non-possessive love. They also speak of the outcome of counselling in terms of growth and healing.[7] We shall, however, throughout this book discover that there is a distinctive mix of interpretation and ritual which makes all Christian ministry distinctive and none more so than that through the occasional offices.

Similar to some ministerial ideals as these notions may be, the counselling presumption may not lightly be made when considering Christian ministry. It represents something deeper in contemporary culture than some may realize. In looking in this direction, the minister may be aligning himself, probably uncritically and almost certainly unwittingly, with the prevailing mores rather than using a culturally neutral stance in the service of his ministry. For example, ministers in busy churches sometimes describe the evening when they are available as their 'surgery'. They are not unique: politicians and others do the same. But it is worth reflecting what model is being suggested as describing the role of the minister and of those who come for an occasional office. The minister's attitude and the words used to describe it convey messages to those who come which may not be intended. But by their sheer continuance the occasional offices

seem to represent a desire for some rite which is precisely
not some cultural norm. To come to the minister for the
performance of a rite and then find oneself caught up
with another 'expert', like the doctor, or the marriage
guidance counsellor, or the school adviser, may be a
diminishing experience which is contrary to the main
thrust of the gospel.[8] The minister may covertly encourage
such encounters, because the apparent stability of the
therapeutically ordered culture may itself be a romantic
longing for control or power.[9] But if this were exposed
and labelled 'Christendom' or 'triumphalism', he would
shun it.

The confidence of the minister in the Christian gospel
has in this argument to be assumed as his primary motivation for ministering. When, however, he meets those
who have specific expectations of one particular role, such
as that of vicar, he also requires some confidence in that
role. That in turn derives from his belief in the church,
not as a theological construct or as an idealized divine
institution, but as a human organization. The occasional
offices bring him face to face with earthy realities of human
beings, the day-to-day church, and above all himself. A
further danger of the counselling presumption is that he
may use it as a defence against these legitimate pressures
upon him and upon his ministry. What may be valuable
in awakening human sensitivity in the minister and
acuteness in listening to what is being conveyed to him,
may become not so much a tool in service of his ministry,
but its substance.

At a practical level, too, the counselling presumption
may make the minister less effective in ministry through
the occasional offices. In therapy the emphasis is upon
listening, time and depth. A series of meetings is more
usual than one brief encounter. There is also the need to
see through a complete process. And, most importantly,
this model assigns prime importance to the one-to-one
meeting. But, as will be seen, although instances of
ministry through the occasional offices sometimes present themselves as such encounters, they are rarely, if
ever, so. They are always social events, and crucial to this
ministry is the institutional role of the church and of its
ministers. The person requesting some such rite comes to
a church or minister which is believed to be handling not

only the realities of existence but also the meaning of life itself and its ultimate significance. The minister's role, therefore, is largely assigned to him, and is one which on the whole he does not determine and which cannot be aligned with those of other 'experts'. For the minister, therefore, the occasional offices will be problematic moments of ministry. They challenge not only theology and professionalism but also the understanding of the gospel and human sensitivity. And however experienced the minister may be, these feelings do not decline. John Taylor, the former Bishop of Winchester, describes how in his last year of office his gardener invited him and his wife to their son's baptism. The family was not familiar with what was going on, but the vicar conducted an excellent service. The bishop and his wife were present in the congregation as guests. Afterwards the bishop wondered whether they should pop in to tea. His wife felt that, as they had not been invited, they might seem intruders at a family occasion. So they did not go. Next day the gardener said how sorry they were that the bishop had not attended the party.

> I came to see that what we are asked to perform is *their* ritual, and if we are prepared to do that as one of the still surviving rituals of our society, then we can claim the right to say 'can we tell you what *we* see in this?' and to explain the deeper Christian understanding of this ritual. . . . the Church is entitled to its 'space', but it is not in the business of expanding its space at the expense of the world.[10]

Indeed, there is always a danger that the church may come to believe that change is happening faster than it realizes. It is then panicked into altering its stance and activity. The way in which new, liturgically accredited but pastorally inept initiation rites have been adopted is an example of this. For all the difficulty that they present, the occasional offices are for the minister the touchstone of ministry, standing as they do at key points of inter-action between the church and its human environment.

We may now turn briefly to the way in which the applicant regards this brief encounter. Later the particular instances will be examined in more detail; here we merely

note some generally observable facets of these engagements. First, it is a request that something be done *for*
them. The preposition is significant: it is not something
done *with* them or *to* them, but is done on their behalf.
This is a key insight, if the church is not to fall into self-
aggrandisement in this area. Rites are not given for all
time. They change in the light of cultural circumstances,
even though the change is slow and hard to perceive.
Rites of passage are transition rites, usually associated
with major moments in human social movement.[11] Given
expression through religious ritual they seem almost
immutable. But these rites do change. For example, for
some marriage has ceased to be regarded as such a rite. It
has been replaced by the acquisition of a mortgage and
the birth of the first child. The ritualizing of living at
home, moving through marriage to setting up a new
household is a comparatively recent development in
Western Europe. Today the 'norm' may be that the couple
sets up house together and maybe gets married later,
sometimes when children are involved. In a curious way,
therefore, the older Christian association of marriage with
procreation is being affirmed in an unexpected fashion.
Such a change confronts the church's believed traditional
teaching. But the pastor will always beware of simplistic
notions of 'tradition' when people's lives are concerned.
It may be, for example, that contemporary concern about
the family is a response to the aggressive, competitive
individualism of industrial capitalism. The church, therefore, or any other body engaged in ritual, does not create
the rite. It has rather to be alert to the nature of the request
that it perform something for people.

The minister's experience of the occasional office is of
a one-off event, which is extracted from people's everyday life and with which they seem to burden the church.
From the applicant's point of view, however, the vision is
different. The ceremony is one event in a continuing
process. What for the minister is a brief line in a full
diary is, for those concerned, almost a timeless moment.
It links in a series of other such moments in the family
history, sometimes almost as if there had been no inter-
vening period. It is intriguing, for example, to note how
each ceremony is often contrasted and compared with
similar occasions which date back through family history.

The photograph album (and maybe now the film and video) has replaced the family Bible as a chronicle. But there is still the record. For baptisms an old christening robe may be brought out, and weddings often have the bride wearing something handed down through the family. Vicars are recalled long after with favour or disfavour. To appreciate this a distinction may be drawn between temporal, or diary, time and experienced time. They are qualitatively different, and the minister who fails to perceive this may find himself operating with the wrong time-scale and feel the associated dislocation.

A second aspect of these brief encounters is the way in which, however humble the occasion, it seems to indicate a sense of something more. A man comes to the cathedral dressed in motor-cycling gear. From his leathers he produces a delicate gold cross, not a cheap one, and asks me to bless it. It is to be given to a girl—not his girl-friend—as a memento of her boy-friend, who was killed in a crash. When we talk—inevitably briefly—many issues arise: genuine affection for the dead friend, whom he can now only contact through the man's closest friend, the girl; a concern for the girl, lest she should feel that no one cares; some vague feeling in himself of the need to express the worth of his own life; and against all these (and no doubt many other issues) the pervasive background of the nearness of death, even to a young man in his twenties. Why should the cross be blessed? Somewhere he dredges up the view that this is right and proper and that the cross has something to do with death. But beyond that he can only be inarticulate. But the major step for him was to come into a cathedral, ask for a priest, have one summoned, and then talk to him.

Similar requests arise over exorcism and the blessing of houses. The line here narrows between full-blown spiritism, from which most people recoil, and a simple belief that there is something 'there' and that it has to be acknowledged. Such ministry calls for authoritative (not authoritarian) action from the pastor. How this is exercised will necessarily vary according to specific circumstances; that it is exercised is essential for ministry. What all these have in common, however, is the sense of some ultimate in the midst of life. There is a human need to be able to 'name something'.[12] If this were not possible,

then life would degenerate into an undifferentiated con-
tinuum. In the face of this prospect, however, the longing
for order, feeble though the grasp of it may be, underlies
much human behaviour. There is a link between this and
the Christian gospel, but to understand this ministers
need to acknowledge theologically what is being interpreted through the contemporary human sciences.

Thirdly, from the applicant's point of view the key to
any encounter over the occasional offices is the rite itself
and the ritual that accompanies it. Ritual consists of for-
malized acts which express things through their symbolic
quality.[13] This is why there sometimes appears to be a
disjunction between the expectations of the minister and
those of the people. The minister tends to think that the
liturgy itself, which he controls, is a sufficient symbol.
For people, however, the perspective is different. At the
baptism that John Taylor described:

> For him [the gardener] the drinking of the champagne
> and the cutting of the cake were just as much a part of
> the ritual as the sprinkling of the water. That was for
> him a rather strange part, he could understand the rest.

In all the occasional offices apparently meaningless pieces
of ritual become important: whether the baby cries or
not; numerous additions to the burial service—words, ivy
leaves, postures; and a very clear example from the marriage service—the use of the stole. At the joining of hands
and pronouncement of the marriage there is no rubric
for the binding of the hands with the stole. It is, however,
often done, and has become 'a popular action in the
sense that at this point the congregation leans forward to
watch, then relaxes with an audible sigh'.[14] Such additional
rituals are not meaningless, but they represent the importance that the people invest in ritual for its own sake.
Unless the minister grasps this, then dissatisfaction and
confusion will result for all.

A minister in a church in a new town found he could
not find a second curate. The church was in the evangelical
tradition, and all the candidates felt that their ministry
should be to churches full of people whom they could
offer a teaching ministry. They could not see any special
value in the fifty or so weddings that they would have to

perform each year, not to mention other rites, and the resulting contact with families in the area. They were all unhappy with the expectation of rites. Since the first edition of this book in 1985 such stories have become even more familiar. There are churches where the minister virtually refuses baptism to those who come from the parish. The Church of England's confusion over weddings has probably increased, although it also appears that the number of those wishing to be married in church may have declined. There is also in some places discussion about whether the church's ministers should conduct the funerals of any other than those known to be professing Christians. In each case the argument runs that it is inappropriate, some would say blasphemous, to use Christian language for those who do not or did not make specific Christian profession. The difficulty has been exacerbated by the more blatant language in the new prayer books and liturgies. But it is not just a matter of language: it represents a question of belief about the Christian gospel and how it is to be proclaimed. This story exposes some of the difficulty in appreciating and thinking about the occasional offices. If the church was to remain and work in that area, at work with the gospel among the parishioners, the ministers needed not merely sociological interpretation into the nature and function of rites, but a means of assigning them theological value as a facet of common human experience. Without that, any suggestions on how to perform these rituals are likely to fall on deaf ears, and rightly so. The formation of the minister and his motivation in the light of the church's work in its environment is the crucial factor. It is, therefore, to a short consideration of such issues that we now turn.

Notes

1. Wesley Carr, *The Priestlike Task* (London, SPCK, 1985), ch. 4; B. D. Reed, *The Dynamics of Religion* (London, DLT, 1978), ch. 5; John Habgood, *Church and Nation in a Secular Age* (London, DLT, 1983); G. Ecclestone ed., *The Parish Church?* (London, Mowbray, 1988); E. Bailey ed., *A Workbook in Popular Religion* (Dorchester, Partners Publications, 1986). The Network for

the Study of Implicit Religion, directed by Dr Edward Bailey, produces up to date bibliographies and runs seminars and conferences: The Rectory, 58 High Street, Winterbourne, Bristol BS17 1JQ.

2. D. Hay, *Exploring Inner Space* (Harmondsworth, Pelican, 1982).

3. Daniel Bell, 'The return of the sacred', *British Journal of Sociology* 28 (1977), pp. 419ff. O. Chadwick, *The Secularization of the European Mind in the Nineteenth Century* (Cambridge, CUP, 1975); A. Hastings, *A History of English Christianity 1920-1985* (London, Collins, 1986). R. Gill, *Beyond Decline* (London, SCM, 1988). Gill also offers a fascinating study of how the churches may have themselves contributed to this sense of decline by overbuilding: *The Myth of the Empty Church* (London, SPCK, 1993).

4. Figures for baptism and church attendance are published annually by the Church of England. Because of a change in definitions only those from 1978 onwards can be used for comparison. The infant baptism rate per 1000 live births are 383 (1978), 365 (1980), 347 (1982), 285 (1989), 275 (1990). These may be compared with the attendance rates per 1000 of the population:

Sunday attendance	27 (1980), 24 (1989), 24 (1990)
Easter	47 (1980), 39 (1989), 41 (1990)
Christmas	49 (1980), 41 (1989), 40 (1990)

The Sunday figure is for attendances; those for festivals are communicants.

5. Bell, 'Return', p. 425.

6. Reed, *Dynamics*, especially ch. 7; Carr, *Priestlike Task*, chaps. 1-3. For a theological exposition of such ministry see Wesley Carr, *The Pastor as Theologian* (London, SPCK, 1991).

7. C. B. Truax and R. R. Carkhuff, *Toward an Effective Counselling and Psychotherapy* (Chicago, Aldine, 1967). The overall theme is explored in the volumes in the New Library of Pastoral Care (London, SPCK), notably A. V. Campbell, *Paid to Care? The Limits of Professionalism in Pastoral Care* (1984), M. Jacobs, *Swift to Hear: Facilitating Skills in Listening and Responding* (1985). There is a useful collection of papers in M. Jacobs ed., *Faith or Fear? A Reader in Pastoral Care and Counselling* (London, DLT, 1987).

8. See P. Selby, *Liberating God: Private Care and Public Struggle* (London, SPCK, 1983), pp. 40ff.

9. Carr, *Priestlike Task*, ch. 6.

10. J. V. Taylor, 'Conversion to the world' in Ecclestone, *Parish Church?*, p. 134.

11. Two seminal works are A. van Gennep, *The Rites of Passage*

(ET London, RKP, 1960) and V. Turner, *The Ritual Process* (London, RKP, 1969). There are also interesting essays in M. Gluckmann ed., *Essays on the Ritual of Social Relations* (Manchester, Manchester University Press, 1962).
12. K. Bliss, *The Future of Religion* (Harmondsworth, Pelican, 1969).
13. J. Beattie, 'On understanding ritual' in B. Wilson ed., *Rationality* (Oxford, Blackwell, 1970).
14. D. L. Barker, 'A proper wedding', in M. Corbin ed., *The Couple* (Harmondsworth, Pelican, 1978), p. 73.

THREE

Rites and the Church's Task

There is a well-known series of pictures which, depending on how they are viewed, convey different images—an old woman or a beautiful demi-mondaine; a snow-covered mountainside or the face of a man; and, probably best known of all, a duck or a rabbit. They are used to distinguish between 'seeing' and 'seeing as'. This distinction is useful for understanding aspects of the church's day-to-day ministry. No human encounter is ever as simple as it first appears. Pastors, therefore, need to be able to perceive as best they may what is being asked and expected from them, if they are not to disappoint, annoy or, at worst, damage people. For some ministers this requires training; others seem to do it naturally. But the point of reflection is the same for all. This chapter is about 'seeing as', using this as an approach to investigating what appears familiar. The focus of study is the outer framework of the pastor's ministry. His inner motivation and theological resource we shall examine in the next chapter. The argument is not a series of hints on how to manage pastoral encounters, but rather it offers a way of interpreting evidence, which may enable the minister to respond to the expectations of those who approach him. A way of analysing pastoral ministry is proposed, particularly as this concerns the occasional offices.

Care, however, is needed with the idea of analysis. It may lead to a form of reductionism, by which people are dehumanized into cyphers. The unexpressed effect is to preserve the integrity of the minister or the believed sanctity of the church. The outcome, then, might be a self-regarding stance which is alien to the gospel. Careful analysis, however, can help ministers to place themselves and the people in a context and so be specific about the task of ministry. One well-known instance is found in work done on bereavement. Several researchers have discerned four major stages to this process: shock, control, regression and adaptation.[1] The value of this analysis for the minister is that it provides a framework within which to try and set the distracting experiences of the bereaved and thus hold some sense of reality on their behalf. But two obvious dangers emerge. First, the minister may take the analysis as a basis of a technique and as a result may reduce in his own mind any individual bereavement to part of a prede-termined process. Second, when they are unsure of what else to say or do, ministers might be tempted to expound this framework to the bereaved person in order to offer reassurance and comfort—'You are not unique'. Against the first approach stand the arguments of the authors themselves that every bereavement is necessarily unique; and against the second we may set the gospel message that life and death are more than conformity to any process. But in spite of such obvious pitfalls such an analysis can profitably inform the minister, not least because at a point of stress it may enable him to recall that human experience is something other than merely the presentation of symptoms.

There are three parts to the argument of this chapter. First, the question is examined as to why people approach the church for such ministry. The occasional offices are chiefly moments when those with fringe or apparently no involvement with the church arrive expecting some service. Even in modern Britain the figures remain significant.[2] Some enquiry into the phenomenon, therefore, is needed. To dismiss it as superstition may not suffice. Second, we shall consider human life in terms of transitions. Third, a model will be offered for analysing the interaction between church and people as a way of giving shape to that which often appears to be unmanageable.

Church and People

Why people come to church remains a mystery. Ministers know that even the most committed member of a congre-gation may apparently on a whim leave, join another church or cease to worship at all. The reason why those with little overt connection with the church approach it for the occasional offices also defies explanation. Never-theless, the fact that they do is a valuable reminder to ministers and church people generally that the church never defines itself. What people have in their minds remains obscure. But it cannot be discounted. For what the church actually is is generated as ministers (lay and ordained) meet people. Each has an idea in the mind and they are unlikely to be congruent. For instance, the former may affirm to themselves 'We are the body of Christ'. The latter may think of the church as 'St Mary's, where we can get our baby baptised'. The meeting of the two concepts is where the working idea of 'church' is generated.

The term which best describes the attitude of all involved in this meeting is 'dependence'. This does not imply that people feel dependent in the everyday sense of the term. As many pastors know, people coming for the occasional offices quite often claim them as rights. The word is used as a value-free description of the way in which people relate themselves to the idea of the church in their minds. Consultants in one study described it like this: 'There is inevitably an element of childlike dependency in the relationship to the church, and thus to its representatives, in that to some extent they are asked to solve the insoluble, cure the incurable, and make reality go away.'[3]

Dependence is not a description of individual behaviour. It refers to the stance with which people come to the church. For instance, even the most sophisticated rarely know exactly what they want. 'It's the proper thing to do' or 'It's right' are common responses. They may be the bane of the minister. But they sum up incomprehensible feelings which come not just from the individual concerned but from the context of that person's life. They may be influenced by the family, or by being British, or by being part of a local community. In a sense they are often acting more than they can realize on behalf of what is loosely called 'society'. The demise of religion, which was at one time confidently predicted, has not occurred. The continuance of requests for the occasional offices is partly evidence for that. Yet religion is suspect in contemporary society. There is a fear in some communities of being seen to be religious at all. In others the risk is of being too religious. But the problem for people is the same: on the one hand they feel some inner pressure to express their dependence religiously and so come to the most obvious place for that—the church. On the other hand they know that such expression is often socially suspect. A step back to naivety ('Because it's right') is, therefore, to be expected rather than reviled.

Such an interpretation could clearly be a form of wish-fulfilment on the part of the clergy to reassure themselves that, in spite of the apparent decline in religious observance, they nevertheless still stand for something important. The evidence needs constant testing. But many, and not the clergy alone, are still surprised by the inexplicable feelings which seem to arise around such events as weddings or funerals. Other material comes from parishes in which the church has pursued a rigorist baptismal policy. Various aspects of ministry in the community appear to have been inhibited because of the anger which becomes diffused throughout the parish, not only among those with babies and children, but more generally. We shall examine this in detail later, but it is worth noting that in such places clergy often use hostile language when referring to their parishioners, while they seek personal gratification and professional legitimation within an eclectic congregation. This observation derives from an Anglican perspective, but so far as I can judge from colleagues in other churches, similar instances can be found elsewhere. But even this behaviour, whether approved of or not, evidences the fundamental point that the church exists by interaction with its human, emotional environment. This relationship is characterized by dependence, as this has been outlined, and this foundation undergirds the following arguments in this book.[4]

Transitions

Shakespeare's Jaques describes seven ages for men, as they journey from distress to momentary glory and finally to 'mere oblivion', playing their brief parts on the world's stage: infant, schoolboy, lover, soldier, ruler, old man, and corpse.[5] Graduation from one stage to the next is not marked by a special rite of passage. They are taken as self-evident progressions, *mutatis mutandis*, for every human being. But the idea lying behind this description of ordered development runs deep in the psyche. Shakespeare's dramatic outline may usefully be compared with that offered by the psychoanalyst Erik Erikson.[6] For Shakespeare the progression is through a series of marked points. Erikson indicates that these historical moments are related to a continuing, and sometimes repeated, series of points of growth, as the individual becomes more aware of his identity.

For example, the birth of a child is an event which has to be named in the life history of that child, of the parents, of the extended family, and so on. The birth also marks a profound shift in the relationship of the parents. It changes from that of a couple to one of a trio. New relationships are created which will affect a series of subsequent, and at the time unknowable, connections. So of Martin Luther, Erikson points out how the way the father and mother related to their son affected the individual personality of the boy. But it did more: it also had an impact on future relationships between Martin Luther and others, including himself and God.[7] Any rite, therefore, which marks a natural transition, also has to take into account that it is dealing with facets of the less conscious and less easily perceived issues of the future. A wedding, baptism or funeral may seem discernible for what it is; almost any number of simple descriptions may be offered. But underlying all are more nebulous, but no less significant, factors. To work effectively in such a context ministers need a model by which to hold and interpret what may be happening.

The idea of 'transition' provides such a model. The two primary transitions in human life are birth and death. In one we come to be; in the other we cease. They govern our ends, in both senses of that term—moments of existence and of significance. These two—existence and meaning— are inseparable, and are acknowledged as such through rites. When, for example, Bede described life as like a sparrow flying through a great hall, coming from the unknown and going to the unknown, he was not merely alluding to life's brevity. He was also drawing attention to the question of its meaning. The two ultimate boundaries to life frame our human development. For example, the way in which birth and the early years determine aspects of our growth is now well known. It is less obvious that the inevitable ending in death is also prefigured in many moments of life.[8] But in every transition, these two ultimate conditions have their effect. For each transition is a moment of birth, newness and opportunity, and death, the ending of the previous state. How we handle birth and death, therefore, affects many moments of our life.

When we face such transitions, we are dealing with life's meaning for individuals and for their human contexts—family, relations, and society in general. We may consider this in terms of rites. If we acknowledge the importance of some sort of closing ritual around death and departure (and this seems widely unquestioned), what might be the forms of rites for acknowledging the proximate boundaries or transitions in life? Historically these have been moments of social significance: puberty, when a child becomes a responsible member of society, or marriage, when the future is acknowledged and, although this may be overlooked, by implication the ending of the parents' life is noted. No doubt in various societies different minor rituals may be observed. Schools, for example, often have entry rituals, both official and unofficial. Less tangible cultural rituals also exist to mark ageing. Each transition, however marked, is characterized by hope for the future and at the same time by some little death. All such rites touch something deeper than is immediately apparent on any specific occasion. How a church, therefore, acts with its rites is important. For historical and cultural reasons the church is seen to make available powerful symbols. It is still expected to use them as it provides certain rites. It may be, therefore, although there seems no way actually to test this, that what the church does may affect society and people within it more than is immediately obvious. For the symbols which the church uses are archetypal.[9]

Over a period of time some rites become more prominent and some less. We have already noted the way in which the informal rite of the first mortgage has appeared. Some rites also decline. We may, for example, discern a steady trend away from confirmation, which was a Christian form of puberty rite. Fewer adolescents are being confirmed. It is difficult to determine precisely why this is so, but the instance is illuminating. The church —at least, the Church of England—has during this period of decline in the number of adolescent confirmations been preoccupied with centralizing its liturgical life on the

Eucharist and discussing rites of initiation. Having encouraged family attendance at the communion service, it has confused the 'normal' progression from Sunday School to confirmation class to participation in the Holy Communion. At the same time theological studies of baptism have exposed the anomalies in confirmation, and consequently the church seems to lack conviction about this particular rite. But this change has not come about in isolation. It has occurred just as the idea of adolescence has become prominent in society. Physical and believed emotional maturity seems to develop earlier and there are consequential changes in social mores. Nor should we underestimate the way in which one group in a society may take up aspects of that society's confusions and uncertainties on behalf of all. Adolescents tend to be blamed for faults which do not strictly or solely belong to them. Putting all this together we may observe that a rite of transition from childhood into adulthood has been diminished, not solely for reasons of theological insight, but also because of changes in the society of which the church is part. Confirmation as a rite has little social impact. There is now no obvious point of entry into adulthood. As an internal and restricted rite of the church confirmation has declined.

This example opens up an important issue for the church and for the occasional offices: who manages such transitions and their accompanying rites? The church has often believed that it controlled them. During the era of Christendom the priest encouraged others to believe, and probably believed himself, that he directed the rite and the person's destiny. But even then the church had to acknowledge that it was possible to be born and to die without a clerical ritual. And in the contemporary world it seems probable that people will increasingly choose how to manage both the proximate and the ultimate boundaries. What also seems likely, however, is that some rites—maybe as yet unfamiliar and unknown—will develop. And if the church withdraws from this area, other agencies will arise. The issue, however, is complicated. While the USSR existed as a unified communist state, secular rituals were created. These seem to have enabled people to handle those transitions which, prior to the revolution, were managed through the church.

Their style was imitative. With the collapse of the Soviet Union, however, the churches, especially the Orthodox, have again been given public recognition. Some of the old rites have been revived, although it is as yet unclear exactly what is happening. This episode is instructive and a warning to the church and its ministers. It seems that in spite of the decline of religious practice in a society which confessed itself to be secular, many people still held a sort of natural religion which sought ritual interpretation of key moments in life. But it also warns against any tendency to think in terms of controlling a profound dimension of people's lives. In all such rites, the celebrants are chiefly the people involved. This is technically true of marriage, as we shall discuss later. But it is in practice the case in all such occasional offices.

A useful concept for thinking about transitions and the occasional offices is that of the 'transitional object'. Most parents are familiar with the doll or bit of rag or other object without which a child will not settle and to which she turns for comfort in distress. No substitute will do. The object is all, until one day, without warning, it is discarded. In developmental terms the child uses this object to make a transition into the beginnings of managing her own life as an individual. She uses it to move from her necessary dependence on her parents into some sense of independence. Eventually the well adjusted child grows into the adult stance of interdependence. To any observer the doll or bit of rag is no more than that. But to the child it is for a while vital.[10]

The significance of the occasional offices for people's lives becomes clearer when we think of them as a sort of transitional object. The ritual naming of a transition—a birth or a death, for instance—acknowledges that it is both very important for our internal life and at the same time it is something outside us. This is exactly a transitional object: it exists outside the child, but what it significantly is may only be felt by the child herself. When as an adult she faces, say, a birth, she may use the objective nature of the rite as a way of orienting her own inner feelings. As a result she will recover a sense of her own self and be able to pick up the new social relationships now demanded.

From this perspective on the rituals of the occasional offices as transitional objects, three points may be noted.

First, if the rite accompanying the transition is seen as the individual's transitional object, it becomes clear that it belongs to them and is invested with meaning by them. The discussions on rites of passage, following van Gennep, open our eyes to social functioning. But for the minister they may obliterate the dynamic aspect of the demand being made on him. These rites do not exist in a vacuum: they belong to the people involved. The minister may be used by people as part of the creation of their temporary transitional object. For the minister, therefore, a crucial question is the theological one: Is such use a legitimate function for the Christian church and for its ministers? This will be examined in a subsequent chapter. Here we merely note that this question cannot be answered by imposing a range of theological assumptions and expectations on the person who requests the ritual.

Secondly, there are inevitably going to be at least three levels of investment in the rite on the part of the applicant. One is historical. A birth, for example, is the beginning of a new life and of changed relationships. It occurs at a point in time; it affects society; it, therefore, is marked in various fashions. Secondly, however, there are underlying psychodynamic aspects, of which those involved will be largely unaware. They will, however, appear to be persistent about things being right and proper, whatever explicit content the minister might wish to introduce. But thirdly, if we take the notion of transitional object into account, we have to add the necessarily irrational and improbable (to the minister) investment that people make. Here it is worth holding to the memory of the child's idiosyncratic behaviour with her transitional object. This is both evidence that irrational behaviour is to be expected and a reminder that it is not, however it may appear, an end in itself but a contributory factor to a total process.

There follows, thirdly, from this one of the hardest points for any minister to appreciate: the process of the ritual is more important than the content. Christians are preoccupied with the meaning of words. They expound and argue over Scripture. They are acutely sensitive about the wording of promises and then become casuistical about the terms used. When, therefore, they are confronted by someone seeking a ritual expression of a transition in their life, ministers become agitated about the words used and the promises made. But for the applicant these are rarely the issues. The church and its minister are a resource for the expression of whatever the people are trying to express. An instance, which will be considered later, is the way in which an offered service of blessing for a child is felt to be unacceptable because it lacks both water (the archetypal symbol) and godparents. And, whatever words are spoken, the applicants will, if deprived of what they expect, often in their minds change what was offered. In one parish the vicar refused all baptisms and would only perform thanksgivings and blessings. After a period of shock and anger, the parishioners were heard to be saying that, whatever the vicar may have said, the service really was a baptism and that their children had been properly initiated.

The minister is engaged in a process over which he has far less control than he might think. The words used and acts performed, although they might momentarily salve his conscience, are not as significant for the people as he might hope. The issues facing ministers are both personal and theological. The question is not how they can capitalize on these opportunities for evangelism, for teaching, or for some similarly forlorn hope. It is whether they can be involved in this aspect of common human experience as ministers of the gospel. But before addressing these questions, I turn to the third approach to developing a way of understanding the interaction of church and society.

Process and Systems

All the participants in the occasional offices experience confusion of some kind. The minister may have an idea of what his church stands for and what the latest policy guideline from the bishop or others proposes. He is also assailed in other roles than that of minister—father, husband, and naturally, another human being. He is caught between upholding the gospel and the church's discipline and at the same time an instinctive affection for ordinary people, without which he can scarcely be Christ's minister. Similar confusions are found with the applicants. They vaguely know what they want but usually cannot articulate it very clearly. Possibly only one of the couple comes

Brief Encounters

about baptism or a wedding, thus expressing something about either cultural or personal expectations of the relationship between them. They, too, carry other roles, since they represent more than they can know. They are trapped between doing what they feel is proper and what they instinctively feel is odd—going to the church and vicar. They feel that it is their church, but they know that in a sense, since they do not attend, it may not be. They almost certainly have residual senses of guilt and are, therefore, wary of the minister and what he may demand. And the prevailing consumer mentality by which most people live tells them that there is nothing in this world that can be acquired for nothing.

Such confusions are endemic in human relationships and, when we reflect on them, we may recognize that it is desirable that they should be, if we are to retain the richness and diversity of human life. But at the moment of encounter, both for the minister and for the applicant, there is no opportunity for such philosophizing. Things have to be dealt with, and usually with speed. For this a framework for interpreting the encounter is valuable. We have already considered how the expectations may be viewed and how the event itself may be appreciated. We turn, therefore, to interpreting the process itself. This is larger than a one-to-one meeting.

When, for example, the minister and a couple discuss the whys and wherefores of a wedding, they are not the only people involved. Each brings with him or herself a crowd of persons who continue to influence them. Some of these are known and may be discussed, such as the family, and many remain unknown, for example, society. The whole range cannot be understood, but it is important for the minister to be aware of it, as she tries to assist, guide, enable, and interpret. Yet they are as weighty imponderables for her as they are for the couple. She does not have superior knowledge. One way, therefore, of being able to hold to the perspective demanded by all this evidence is to work with a framework. By this means a minister may be freed from a preoccupation with the niceties of the couple's questions and can thus begin to enable them to explore the specific issues of marriage which face them. At the same time she is able to minister by providing a means of shaping the mass of confusions in which they find themselves.

Systems thinking provides such a framework. It makes us think of institutions and organizations in terms of their basic activities. All of them take things in, do something with them, and produce an output. An animal, for example, can be viewed in this way. It takes in food, sensory perceptions and so on, converts them to sustain its life, and leaves both waste (a by-product) and, more significantly, its impact on its environment. Or again, an industrial company has a range of inputs—materials, personnel, enthusiasms, finance—which it converts into products, pay, a contented workforce, dividends. Two points emerge from these simple illustrations. First, most systems are far more complicated than they initially appear. The industrial company, for instance, will be in trouble if its management thinks of its function solely in terms of converting raw materials into manufactured goods. If the human throughput is ignored, trouble ensues. Second, the focus of thinking on a systems model is on the way in which the organization or organism acts and reacts with its context. The focus of attention and interpretation, therefore, becomes the specific point of such interaction.[11]

This model is instructive when used of the occasional offices. An immediate thought may be to think of the church as the system. The input is people's confusion; the conversion is sorting it out and, when appropriate, deploying ritual resources; and the output is some sort of more fulfilled people. In such a system the minister would have a managerial role on behalf of the church, enabling people to pass through the total process. But this is a false view, not least as an interpretation of the occasional offices. People who come for a ritual in one sense do not need the church. They are managing their own lives and will do so, whether the church is involved or not. They turn to the church not for management but for opportunity. What needs regulation is the interchange between the people concerned and the social, psychological and family environments in which they are set. In the many interlinked strata of experience there is bound to be confusion between what is the system and what the environment. But the applicants themselves manage. The input is a series of feelings, some of which they know and some of which seem incomprehensible. The conversion is the process by which these are sorted and interpreted, so that the people concerned may better locate themselves in life with themselves, their families, their neighbours, and, Christians will add, with God. The output is human beings or new human units (marriages or families) which can sustain a vision of life having some meaning for themselves and for others. The church and its ministers serve that process. They do not control it.

Uncomfortable as this perception may be, it is fundamental as an insight into Christian ministry. For ministers it has particularly important consequences. It implies that responsibility for what happens through an occasional office does not rest with them or the church. But the pain of the confusions, the inadequacy of the experiences, and the necessarily unfulfilled nature of human life, remain with the minister. But through this he may, as part of his own vocation, carry an enlarged vision of what is happening and an image of God's grace and involvement in human life. That is Christian ministry. In order to perform this task, the idea of a system is a useful heuristic tool for giving the minister a point at which to latch on to the human experience of the applicant. It also enables him to enable the encounter to take place where it matters most for those who approach him. But it also, by holding to the primary notion of the church as having a task within its environment and the minister having a role in relation to that task, pushes ministers firmly towards their grasp of the grace of God, upon which their ministry ultimately rests.

Notes

1. E. Kübler Ross, *On Death and Dying* (London, Tavistock, 1970); C. M. Parkes, *Bereavement* (Harmondsworth, Pelican, 1972); Y. Spiegel, *The Grief Process* (ET London, SCM, 1978). For specific reference to ministry to the dying and bereaved see I. Ainsworth-Smith and P. Speck, *Letting Go* (London, SPCK, 1982).
2. See Chapter 2, n. 4.
3. W. G. Lawrence and E. J. Miller, in E. J. Miller, *From Dependency to Autonomy* (London, Free Association Press, 1993). See also Reed, *Dynamics* and Carr, *Priestlike Task passim.*

4. See Wesley Carr, 'Irrationality and religion', in J. Krantz and D. Lofgren eds., *Authority, Irrationality and Work* (New York, APA, forthcoming).
5. *As You Like It*, Act 2, Scene 7.
6. E. H. Erikson, *Identity and the Life Cycle* (New York, Norton, 1980), ch. 2. A useful discussion of these ideas may be found in R. Stevens, *Erik Erikson* (Milton Keynes, Open University, 1983).
7. E. H. Erikson, *The Young Man Luther* (London, Faber, 1959).
8. The major work in this field is J. Bowlby, *Attachment and Loss*, 3 vols. (London, Hogarth, 1969-80).
9. See C. G. Jung, *Man and his Symbols* (ET London, Jupiter, 1964).
10. For references and a full discussion of the pastoral and theological implications of this concept, see Carr, *Pastor as Theologian*, especially pp. 21ff.
11. E. J. Miller and A. K. Rice, *Systems of Organization* (London, Tavistock Press, 1967).

FOUR

The Priority of Grace

In the Christian tradition, from the time of the New Testament onwards, pastoring and teaching go hand in hand. The pastor is always a theologian, not someone who, as it were, does the work and is kept up to the mark by someone else, who is a theologian.[1] The occasional offices open up a distinctive range of theological issues, especially the theology of sacraments. Because these offices are related to transitions in life and employ natural symbols they also invite us specifically to consider the way that God relates to his world, especially the messiness of human life. Some ministers seem to look for certainty in their theology so as to deal with the problems presented by these offices. Others find their confidence in the fact of this ministry and leave the confusion in their theology.

Any survey of the occasional offices will demonstrate that they have changed in the course of time. In one sense a baptism, wedding or funeral remains a rite. But what is expected of it and invested in it continually changes. Baptism is a key instance, since it focuses many of the discomforts about the church's ministry through the occasional offices. But even this most Christian of rituals is affected by people's expectations of the church. The Church of England, for example, has customarily baptized the babies of any parishioner who asks. Some clergy wish to reject this policy on the grounds that it is a betrayal of the Christian gospel in today's climate. Yet even this position comes about because of the way that the church and people interact. It is not a 'pure' theological stance.[2] Marriage presents a similar difficulty for all churches, especially over the issue of divorce and remarriage. To some the words of Jesus seem clear and prescriptive. Others read them differently. But few, if any, doubt that the concept of what marriage is has changed since the time of Christ.[3] Death might seem to be immutable. But its significance and how it is faced continue to change.[4] Funerals, as is often remarked, are not what they were.

In all three instances, therefore, pastors are faced with pressure upon the way in which the church which they represent affirms its own identity. In one sense a baptism is a baptism, and always has been. Yet the scantiest knowledge of history demonstrates the importance of the context in determining the theology. If infant mortality is the norm, then early and urgent baptism to protect the infant soul from damnation dominates thinking. Such views remain even today, although they do not predominate. Indeed there is some evidence that baptism might be sometimes delayed until a second child is born and then the rite becomes something to do with consolidating the family unit. The theological point is that every reinterpretation of baptism also constitutes a reinterpretation of the church. And that process throws up questions about the nature of that church, its identity and continuing faithfulness to the gospel. Such questions are more uncomfortable in a pluralist society with its ready drift towards relativism.

Among the response to these pressures we may discern trends in the life of the church which affect our topic. Beneath many of the ecumenical explorations today lies the question of whether a pluralistic world requires a variety or plurality of churches or whether it needs one church to stand for an idealized community amid social fragmentation. Or again, with the many problems of authority which abound in the world, it is not surprising that the churches become preoccupied with authority as an issue and begin to look for simple solutions. The fundamentalisms—itself a partisan term of abuse—whether biblical, ecclesiastical or historical, become dominant in the life and thinking of all churches.[5] All these affect approaches to the basic issue of the church's identity.

There is one more stance which is a common aspect of human behaviour and which has to be taken into account in any thinking about the church and its environment—projection.[6] This term describes the way in which individuals and groups dispose of aspects of their selves, usually those which are disturbing or distressing, by projecting them into others and then dealing with them there. When facing issues which raise questions about the church's identity, special care is required, if we are not to project the church's problems and uncertainties on to others and then blame them. Among the 'others' who are most available for this are those who, for whatever reason, request the occasional offices. If we are to think about the theology which might illuminate and be illuminated by such a ministry, we have to take into account this danger as well as the question of the church's identity.

The identity of Christianity is a contentious issue. Stephen Sykes has indicated the problems that afflict people when trying to think of essence or identity, but maintains that the church still has to make the attempt to discover a specific way of speaking about its unity over time, which is not open to obvious objection. Continuity itself is always assumed. It is indeed impossible to conceive anything that might be termed 'Christianity' which did not claim continuity with the past and particularly with Jesus Christ. But once the attempt is begun, one slips either into a sort of theological blinkers, which allow unaccommodating material to be ignored, or into cultural relativism, or into so wide a definition of Christianity that it embraces everything and therefore claims nothing. Sykes suggests that we enquire under what conditions Christianity might be grasped as one thing. His solution is that Christianity is a contested concept, which is expressed in a series of propositions. Some of these are external to experience and take the form of the basic Christian stories. The other form is internal, relating to the experience of Christian people in each generation. Between the story and the experience there is a continuing and continuous interaction, from which Christianity derives its identity.[7]

This proposal offers a way to explore applied or pastoral theology. Whereas Sykes locates the contest between the external and internal aspects of Christianity within the church, we might alternatively suggest that it is examined between the church and its environment.[8] Some, following this idea, might see the church as holding the stories to which the world might bring its experiences. In the contest between them truth might emerge for all concerned. Such a view is not wholly improbable, but it has tinges of an unattractive triumphalism, which is alien to the incarnational basis of the primary story which the church holds. A better alternative is to reverse the question. We may regard people in the world as holding their own stories and forms of belief. We shall never fully know where they get them from and how they are conditioned. They make up what people call religious experience. By contrast, the church holds to the vitality of the experience of God. But it cannot do this in isolation from the world. So when general religious experience (people's stories) and specific Christian experience come together change occurs in both. At its highest that change in someone's story constitutes conversion. In the encounter the church's experience is also changed. The experience of such meeting and change is also likely to be, as Sykes points out, conflictual. Since this engagement is a two way interaction, not a one way conveying of a message or demand, the twin errors of triumphalism and relativism are excluded.

This generalized theory may be studied specifically through the instance of infant baptism. Baptism is a boundary event. That of an infant is associated with the entering the world. It is also about regeneration, crossing a boundary from one world to another, or incorporation, joining one group and leaving another. Whether all this is understood and grasped by the participants is not at issue here. As a rite baptism is a function of the perceived or believed boundary of the church, which may at times align itself with a similar boundary in common human experience—that of birth. Thus any theology of baptism that does not start from interaction across these boundaries will be deficient in theological and pastoral content. Baptisms are performed, and the act of doing cannot be separated from the understanding which underlies it and is developed through it. This is a double interaction between, on the one hand, the Christian story and human experience, and, on the other hand, the particular human story and Christian experience.

For the former there is ample evidence, not least in the form of liturgies. The latter view, however, may be less familiar, and for this we have to examine some of the images of baptism. These are a series of symbols, chief among which are birth and water. These are powerful natural symbols, which do not belong exclusively to the church. Indeed, the church did (and does) not have a monopoly on baptism as a ritual. The earliest Christians had problems over the similarity of pagan mysteries.[9] Sometimes the church links other symbols—light and fire, as in the connection with the Easter vigil and the paschal fire and today in the more modest suggestion of handing the parents and godparents a lighted candle. However intimately Christians tie their own interpretations to these symbols, their archetypal value and effect will out whenever they are invoked. So, for example, Christians may wish to emphasize dying and rising with Christ as the basic baptismal image. But they cannot eradicate the other associations, such as those of purification and uncleanness or of thirst and pure water. So if we ask whose story we are handling, even in a primary Christian sacrament, we have to acknowledge that it is not exclusively Christian property. These symbols are the possession of human beings and are the church's on loan or by temporary, partial appropriation.

This is not easy for Christians to accept, and the problems that such an insight raises are dealt with within the church obliquely and sometimes roughly. We are told that the church has again entered a pre-Constantinian world, that Christendom (for some a term of abuse) is no more, and that the life of the church is now similar—some would claim almost identical—to that in which the first Christian communities established themselves and developed their faith. But a moment's reflection will expose the error. There is no sense in which the present age may be described as pre-Constantinian. Nor is there very much in common between the first and the twentieth centuries of the Common Era. And although some may delude themselves into thinking that they can experience precisely what their predecessors experienced, most know that this is not possible. All live in a post-Constantinian age which is still affected, and will be, by its response to the fact of Christendom.

A second attempt at handling the problem of baptism as a boundary sacrament is by projection. Within the Church of England, for example, we find disputes about baptismal practice. Groups and individuals are labelled 'indiscriminate' or 'rigorist'. It is doubtful whether there

are or have been many who really baptized indiscrimi-
nately. The act of discrimination is itself qualified by the
historical and cultural context in which it occurs. Equally
'rigorist', with its overtone of ungraciousness, does no
justice to the pastoral intent and effort of those who
appear to restrict baptism. This controversy seems to have
taken over the violence from the previous dispute between
paedobaptists and credobaptists. But the argument is not
primarily about the practice of baptismal administration.
It is fuelled by a range of uncertainties (in spite of the
many claimed certainties) about the identity of the church
and the nature of its engagement with the modern world.

None of these controversies can be resolved by the
usual courts of appeal. This perception itself is a further
contributory cause of the arguments. For Scripture is
notoriously unhelpful in this field. In spite of much study,
which has clarified many points, the modern church is
still not much more enlightened on the question of
infant baptism than the compilers of the Thirty-Nine
Articles. The church's history and traditions compound
the problem. So great is the variety of interpretation during
the first five centuries that almost anything can be, and
is, demonstrated from tradition. From this follows the
inevitable failure of the forlorn hope that liturgiologists
might rescue the church's pastoral practice. That we
know more about the history of baptismal practice
reminds us of the different contexts, both responded to
and created by the church's ministry, which applied in
various eras. Much study has been done on the liturgical
material of the occasional offices. A great deal has been
learned. But the outcome in terms of the theology and
practice of ministry is disappointing. By focusing on
liturgy the churches have tended to find points of agreement, or at least understanding, between themselves. But
the cost has been to shift these offices from the boundary
between the church and its context into the inner life of
the church. The key question has implicitly become: what
do these offices express about the church?

So, for instance, if baptism is regarded chiefly as a
qualification for participation in the Eucharist, then many
of the apparent problems seem resolved by default. It
can be defined as the mode of entry into the community
which celebrates the Eucharist.[10] There is, however,

another effect. The orders of service which result over-emphasize the Christian story, at the expense of that with which people come, and diminish the Christian experience as the point of interpretation. The typological language in the Alternative Service Book 1980 may be liturgically well founded, but the room for the expression of human emotions in baptisms, weddings and funerals is limited.

Because each occasional office, including baptism, is concerned with boundaries, transitions and interpretation, it follows that these will always be points at which the church's understanding of itself will be challenged and modified. Each office is not simply a rite with which the church addresses the world. It also speaks to the church which offers this rite. What the rite is, to whom it is offered, how it is performed, these and similar questions cannot be determined by the church in terms of its present understanding of the gospel alone. For baptism especially, but also marriage and funerals, are not solely a proclamation of the Christian story. They are also announcements about the basic human story of birth, death and transitions between the two. How that is theologically evaluated is as, if not more, important than the history of the rituals and liturgical propriety. The rite, therefore, is never done to people. It can only be performed with them. And the message involved is directed by God as much to the church as to those seeking these occasional offices.

In the light of this approach, we can discern three theological axioms which are fundamental for any thinking about ministry through the occasional offices. They are not the complete theology of such ministry, since, as has been indicated, in the nature of the case that could never be produced. Nor are their implications spelled out in full. That would require a major theological text. Even more, however, if pastors are the theologians, it follows that the detailed theological outworking of such ministry will be continually taking place so long as it is exercised. But these three points provide necessary guide posts for any theology of the occasional offices.

The World is God's

The point is obvious, but if there is any division between mankind in general and Christians in particular at the root of thinking about ministry, then the stuff of experience with which people come to the church will be devalued and ministry will be difficult, if not impossible. Common human experience, especially in the inarticulate form that it takes around these life-cycle events, has to be valued as part of the divine creation. It may then form a basis upon which the meaning of the gospel may be constructed by minister and applicant alike. 'We are all immigrants in the world we now experience.'[11] Significant changes are occurring in our human relationships with our environment and within our societies. As a result, an alienation from these familiar supports has become more important than alienation through economic oppression. There is, however, also an additional sense of isolation. In this technologically driven society people seem to be isolated even from the possibility of divine grace. The apparently simple affirmation, therefore, that the world is God's, leads to a continuing examination of the church's activity.

The vision of Deutero-Isaiah is an excellent scriptural launching-pad for the pastor as theologian. The author proclaims that the apparent tragedies of exile, alienation and isolation bring benefits. The greatest of these is that they enlarge the vision of God, because they link the vision of the natural world to the problems of the political. The writer's sense of God is notably majestic. But he achieves this without correspondingly devaluing common human experience. A key theme is that of God's servant. This servant is not necessarily an obvious agent of God whom the people of God can recognize. He can be unexpectedly anointed, as in the case of Cyrus (Isa. 44:24—45:13).

Reflection on the bold vision of Deutero-Isaiah illuminates the way in which the church and pastor can value every demand for one of the occasional offices because it is a presentation of common human experience. The minister is like the servant. He or she enables people, through the way in which they treat others and in turn allow them to treat the minister, to hold together, examine and gain a new perspective on their present existence. The theme is summed up in the servant song in Isaiah 53.

Little used in the New Testament, this was subsequently seen as a description of the ministry of Christ. That model, too, applies to the ministry of his church in a world which is God's, even if it frequently seems not to be.

Church and World

'Mission' and 'ministry' are often compared and contrasted. But the argument seems false. Whatever the detail, both terms points to one common factor: others. If the task is seen as mission, it draws attention to those to whom Christians go with the gospel. If it is regarded as ministry, it indicates the fact of the other to whom care and teaching are offered. The life of the Christian church is only possible in so far as there are others. These are often described by the shorthand 'the world'.

One of the main ways in which we grow into adulthood and have some sense of ourselves is to become aware not just of I but of Not-I. The earliest grasp of this is as the infant discovers that mother is Not-I. For the rest of our life we populate the world with others who are not us. Sometimes the relationships become pathological and disturbed. But for most purposes this is the normal mode of living.[12] This process is not confined to the individual. The church, for instance, needs the world; without it the church could not identify itself. How the two react with one another is the crucial point of mission and ministry.

It is for this reason that the doctrine of the Holy Spirit is important in any of the church's ministry. Often the Spirit is invoked in terms of authorization. But this is an inadequate view. For both church and world share the same originator, namely God. But where is he to be distinctively discerned? The work of the Spirit is essentially a linking activity. He is therefore to be found in points of contact and the interstices of the varied facets of the divine creation.[13] Such interchanges as there are, therefore, in the occasional offices are prime moments of potential divine revelation. They are also, as points where church and world interact, necessarily where the Spirit is. There are, and no doubt will continue to be, major disagreements among Christians about these offices. In these debates the role of the Spirit is often invoked. But whatever else may be believed, it is essential that

Christians do not implicitly exclude the action of the Spirit from such encounters. To do so diminishes the work of God. It also will reduce the church's capacity to be aware of God and consequently for identifying itself.

Grace is Never Cheap

This theme follows naturally from the previous two. One danger attending the contemporary church is that it may hope to survive by seeking spiritual purity and specific Christian identity. One result is that the messiness of belief and the problems of identifying themselves is projected into others. An instructive parallel may be drawn between these trends to rigorism of belief and membership and early monasticism. That movement, although rigorous and clear in many ways, was flawed because it implied that genuine Christian faith could only be achieved by the few. Under the guise of humble dependence on divine grace there ensued a hunt for merit.[14] But such perfection is not to be found in the compromises and problems of common human experience. Nor is it likely to be discovered within groups of like-minded people, which encourage social and individual narcissism.

The crucial question thus becomes: who will bear the disappointment involved in ministry with ordinary people? It is one thing to present the claims of God to those who seek the performance of the rite. God's grace is not cheap and his presence always carries demands. This we shall examine later. But it is quite another thing, whether wittingly or not, to inflict the cost of grace which the Christian experiences upon vulnerable people who approach the church for some ministry. There are moments when they seem expected to bear the pain of the church's concern with its identity.

In any pastoral encounter is the church to risk its own integrity and, as it might believe, the integrity of God himself? One major difficulty for pastors is that the decision does not ultimately rest with the formal teaching of the church but in their instantaneous judgement. The disciples of Jesus Christ of all people should understand what it is to be used, abused and misused and to endure the resulting distress. Anything other than that is a reversal of the gospel of one who was unjustly killed to no immediately obvious effect.[15] The basis of discipleship, too, is that life is lost when we seek to save it. The true nature of divine graciousness is that, in order to affirm others, even if they are limited or mistaken in their appreciation of God's world, it will risk being misunderstood and misused.

Obviously each of these three points can and must be amplified. That is the theological task of the pastor. But they provide three boundary posts for the church's ministry which cannot be removed. For the Christian they seem to be built into the nature of God himself and the shape of ministry. For that reason they are both necessary and uncomfortable.

Notes

1. See Carr, *Pastor as Theologian* for a full exposition of what this implies for the pastor's theology and practice. The wider question of doctrine in general is addressed by C. Cuncliffe, 'Doctrine, Social Theory and Practice', *Theology* (1989), pp. 25ff.
2. See the discussion in G. Kuhrt, *Believing in Baptism* (London, Mowbray, 1987).
3. The Church of England's struggle on this question is distinctive because of its responsibility as the established church. The material may be found in two reports: *Marriage, Divorce and the Church* (London, SPCK, 1971) and *Marriage and the Church's Task* (London, CIO, 1978). Other churches have also been engaged in a similar debate and published documents.
4. G. Gorer, *Death, Grief and Mourning in Contemporary Britain* (London, Cresset, 1965) remains informative.
5. See R. Gill, *Competing Convictions* (London, SCM, 1989).
6. The term is used here in a general, popularized sense. For a fuller discussion of the importance of projection and projective identification see E. R. Shapiro and A. W. Carr, *Lost in Familiar Places* (New Haven, Yale University Press, 1991). Also Carr, *Pastor as Theologian,* pp. 32ff.
7. S. W. Sykes, *The Identity of Christianity* (London, SPCK, 1984).
8. Wesley Carr, 'A teaching church with a collective mind', *Crucible* (1983), pp. 148ff.

9. Mary Douglas, *Natural Symbols,* rev. edn (Harmondsworth, Pelican, 1973).

10. D. Wright, 'The Lima Report: *Baptism* and *Eucharist* compared', *Theology* 87 (1984), pp. 330ff.

11. M. Hare Duke, *Stories, Signs and Sacraments in the Emerging Church* (London, Mowbrays, 1982), p. 25.

12. For a discussion of this in relation to ministry and theology see Carr, *Pastor as Theologian.*

13. This theme is elegantly outlined in J. V. Taylor, *The Go-Between God* (London, SCM, 1972).

14. For the history see D. J. Chitty, *The Desert a City* (Oxford, OUP, 1966). For an interpretation see D. Bonhoeffer, *The Cost of Discipleship* (ET London, SCM, 1959), pp. 38ff.

15. J. Moltmann, *The Crucified God* (ET London, SCM, 1974). Wesley Carr, *Tested by the Cross* (London, HarperCollins, 1992), and *Pastor as Theologian,* especially chapters 8–10.

FIVE

Christian Sacraments and the Human Life-Cycle

It is impossible to discuss pastoral practice and the occasional offices without reference to the sacraments. The offices themselves are sacraments or quasi-sacraments (the disputes over the number of sacraments is not important here). For ministers, too, the sacraments are one of their major supports in their ministry.

The Eucharist has widely become the key sacrament of the church's life. In part this is the result of a sustained move towards emphasizing the significance of the local congregation. Today's Holy Communion assures worshippers of their identity as the people of God or body of Christ. The underlying theory is that 'as therefore the parish is the local unit of the Church of God, the Parish Eucharist is of necessity the central act of its life'.[1] But an unexpressed belief may also underlie this development. As the churches become less sure of their place in people's minds and so more doubtful about their interaction with their context, they may be creating a stronger sense of their own identity. One result, therefore, is that the churches have been and are moving in an opposite direction to that which many people still expect of them. For the church, both ministers and members, the Eucharist is the focal sacrament. Baptism (the second dominical sacrament) is minimized into the entry rite to the eucharistic community. By contrast, however, for those who bring children for baptism, this is what the church is for, while the Eucharist remains somewhat irrelevant and remote.

This difference of perspective is often observable in practice when baptisms are held in the context of the parish communion. Everyone involved seems to become uncomfortable: the family, who have brought the child, feel trapped into another, alien rite for which they did not bargain; the regular worshippers seem unsure quite how to behave towards those who feel like intruders but whom they do not wish so to regard. And, like the family, the regular worshippers are also caught up in a rite for which they did not bargain, with the emphasis upon congregational participation that is a feature of most modern liturgies. When we see the church and people apparently moving on two such separate planes around the two major sacraments of the church, then some examination of what this means is required.

The theology of sacraments has to be recovered as an aspect of the examination of pastoral practice rather than one of theoretical ecclesiology alone. In all countries where Christianity has become the dominant religion this means facing the issue which is both pastoral and theological. This may be formulated in two inseparable questions. First, what (if any) is the legitimacy of linking Christian sacraments and the human life-cycle? And second, given the historical and cultural facts, are people brought to faith through depriving them of these rituals or not?[2] These two questions take us to the heart of the unavoidable complexities of the occasional offices: the problem of identity for professing Christians; the primacy of liturgy, and hence also ritual, in the churches; the inescapable cultural and historical contexts of the church's life and witness; and the connection between ritual and faith. But ultimately this debate directs attention to a further, more basic question: Do the Christian sacraments belong to the Christian church? In what follows baptism will be used as material for exploring this issue.

Baptism, or a similar rite, may be found in many religions and societies. Some may argue that Christian baptism is qualitatively different from all these and therefore is unique. But if we then resort to the customary Christian approach of studying the history of this peculiar and unique rite of Christian baptism, the question merely emerges under other guises. Although baptism appears very early in the history of Christianity, Christians were not the first to baptize.[3] Jesus' disciples, for example, if they were baptized at all, were probably baptized only with John's baptism. One of the most striking features of this rite in the early Christian centuries is the way in which it seems to have been variously understood and practised. This observation applies to all periods, and not just to the major adjustment which followed the conversion of Constantine. In most cases the theologians who wrote the theology were the bishops who performed the rite. They were largely agreed on a few points—the forgiveness of sins, the gift of the Spirit, and the unrepeatable nature of baptism. But beyond these they spoke of the rite in their own terms. The history of baptism in the first five centuries of the Christian church is one of variety and change. When the creeds mentioned 'one baptism', this could not be interpreted to mean 'one understanding of baptism'. There are two important and continuing reasons for this.

First, theology during this period was regarded as a creative enterprise. The enthusiasm for taking such risks declined, however, as the experience upon which the theologizing was done, the experience of salvation, was separated from the rite of baptism. This followed upon the second main reason for the change: the social context within which the Christian church established itself by interaction. The major adjustment in AD 313, when Constantine formally adopted Christianity, is often noted. Yet this was a comparatively minor event compared with the fall of the Roman empire and the invasion of the Germanic tribes. This dramatically modified the practice and understanding of baptism. It declined as the setting out moment of the Christian pilgrimage (or sometimes its completion). More emphasis was placed, not least through the mass baptisms performed by the missionaries, on initiation into life after death and into the local, social Christian culture. Another facet of sacramental theology is thus disclosed. Far from its being one of the intimate, almost private, aspects of the church's theology and practice, baptism appears as a function of the boundary conditions that exist, or are believed to exist, between the church and its environment. The sacrament itself, therefore, is also adjustable.

This church is not that of the theoretician but that of the practising pastor. In medieval Christendom baptism of infants was the norm. It had little direct link with experience. Spiritual regeneration is fundamental, but it is also necessarily secret. The sacraments become a means to sustain this way of life. The abuses of this system lead to the reformations of the fourteenth to sixteenth centuries. The grace of God, as experienced, again becomes prominent, but the question remains whether it is possible to have that grace without knowing it. Luther found that he had to affirm that this could be the case. Others gave different answers. But in every case the theology and practice of the sacraments were inseparable and were judged to be capable of change.[4]

In modern times a series of new factors appears. The more immediate awareness of non-Christian religions alters the perception of the missionary task. Infant death is less prevalent and the sense of original sin and the need for forgiveness decline in significance. By contrast, however, people categorize themselves and allow themselves to be labelled, as if such labels assign status. New social rituals emerge.[5] And underneath the psychotherapeutic drift of our society lies the need to sustain the illusion that men and women, even if they cannot know God's grace, can at least have the love and mercy of one of their fellow men.[6] The churches also conform to this norm as they emphasize the incorporation of men and women into Christ and into participation in the fellowship of the church. The rite of baptism accordingly changes again, as may, for example, be seen in the new rites of the Church of England with their expressions of welcome and prevailing description of the church as a family.

For all the concern about the church's identity in the world, its behaviour at this ritual of self-identification conforms to the prevailing culture of the society in which it is set. Once more, therefore, we note theological and cultural pluralism coinciding around the sacrament of baptism. Appeals to Scripture, tradition and history, as means either of validating existing practice or authenticating longed-for alternatives, in fact only witness to the richness and variety of meaning to be found in this one Christian sacrament. They also indicate the way in which, functioning as part of the boundary between the church's task and its environment of the world, baptism is bound to change. There can be no appeal away from pastoral practice and demand to an agreed theological position. Theology is created as ministry is practised.

If there is no escape to a purely theoretical stance, there is also no pathway from the dilemmas of ministry through the seductive pastures of liturgy. The revival of liturgical studies has had a profound effect on the contemporary church. Many, if not most, churches have revised their liturgies during the past generation. On the whole they have done so in the same way. Committees were appointed to change the pattern of how people related to God. Research flourished and experts (occasionally frustrated by synods) modified and directed the functions of rituals for the good of those employing them. But something was lost as this happened. Change came about very quickly as 'the long, slow and complex evolutionary process that has always been typical of crucial human patterns, such as language and liturgy, was drastically reduced to less than two decades'. This remark was made about the Roman Catholic Church, but it is true of others.[7] This is a substantial issue and more than querulousness at the supposed or genuine inadequacies of the new services. It indicates an area of difficulty for the minister, especially when he is under stress because of his engagement with superstitions, folk-religion and half-belief. For the liturgical framework which he employs no longer resonates with the half-remembered liturgies which expressed the faintly held beliefs of those who approach him. Not only is this world unfamiliar in language and detail; it is also one which has been framed without reference to them. As a result the minister is caught in a series of binds, which we may list.

1. The applicants for ministry through the occasional offices look to him as one who holds a tradition. This is on the whole a melange within the corporate, folk mind. It is held with vigour and confusion, not least in terms of what is proper and what has 'always been done'. As the minister knows, that 'always' may cover anything, from what happened at a friend's church to what mother says. But the sense of tradition, however vague and inaccurate in detail, is nevertheless strong.

2. The minister is not in fact the repository of these 'traditions'. He holds a Christian tradition, which nurtures

and informs him. His ministry is concerned with negotiation between these two sorts of tradition. But for him to feel confident and competent, his own tradition has to sustain him. When there is a feeling that liturgies are not evolving from worship and pastoral ministry but are arriving from somewhere other than this nub of ministry, the supports of the minister's own Christian tradition are not always effective.

3. As a result of this conflict of traditions, the applicants for the occasional offices do not experience the minister as a reliable bearer of a tradition. He seems less dependable than they believe he ought to be. The people, already to some extent uncertain and guilty, become unsure of the one with whom they are dealing. This uncertainty is felt and is difficult, if not impossible, to articulate. Consequently it is not amenable to rational exploration and discussion. In fact the more talk there is, the more apprehension increases.

4. The minister in turn feels unsure about what he ought to do, his church and tradition appearing uncertain, and unable to grasp precisely what the applicants want, since they are even less confident about him. He is, therefore, in some internal disarray and may fall back on various defences. He may create an apparent certainty about the church and its traditions, making it rigid rather than flexible. He may emphasize understanding at the expense of feeling. Or he may reckon that discussion is too difficult in the circumstances and salve his conscience by giving people a booklet. They in turn depart with something, even if it is only a piece of paper, but also carrying the minister's disarray in them.

5. Those who can negotiate this obstacle course, either through profound interpretation (very few), sudden grasp of the understanding that the minister requires (some in certain social groupings), or through sheer willingness to say and do anything to achieve the required result (many), arrive at their desired end of some sort of ritual.

There is an element of caricature in this outline. But this process returns us to the original question of whether the sacraments belong to the church. The phenomenon of people turning to the church like this cannot merely be dismissed as a remnant of Christendom in a secular world. In all but the very early generations of Christians we find sacramental religiosity among those who do not practise their religion but who cling to a belief that is expressed at moments in the life-cycle.[8] However this may be described, it is an issue for the church and not something to be diagnosed in the applicants and abandoned there. Yet it is no use Christian ministers resigning themselves to being generally religious. They are expected to be Christian. To interpret this engagement and to sustain the minister a Christian theology of sacraments in the context of religion in general, is required.

If religion is viewed not as a peculiar phenomenon of its own kind but as a dimension of common human experience, the Christian approach is to place it in the context of God's creation. That in turn relies upon more than a notion of an original and sustaining act on God's part. It always matches creation with the idea of new creation. Without this connection any interpretation may degenerate into mere religiosity. With it, however, we are taken to the heart of the Christian gospel. For the hope of new creation in Christ is precisely what is proclaimed in the distinctively Christian emphasis upon resurrection. Thinking about creation has been overloaded with ideas of work, rationality and order. Creation is held to be a profitable and useful activity; the world is potentially rational; and somewhere running through everything is a basic order. These ideals have also come to dominate pastoral ministry, with its emphasis upon work and busyness, on the need for understanding, and the longing to impose order on what seems a chaotic experience of ministry. The religious impulse, which presents itself in the occasional offices, desires to go further. Where there is order, there is also the disorder of enthusiasm or superstition, and where there is a sense of the need to work, these people bring in an almost irresponsible gaiety or play.

Resurrection, or new creation, reminds us that all creation is an act of divine choice, whether it is making the world or raising Jesus Christ. Choice, however, is the prerogative of the leisured, those who have choosing time. It does not necessarily have anything to do with work. The story of the resurrection is redolent with play —an empty tomb, which poses a riddle; a mysterious encounter with Mary, like dressing up; the road to Emmaus, a form of blind man's buff. Angels and messages, appearances and joyous confusion mark the resurrection story as one of fun, games and play. Creation and new creation, the vision of mankind and the free play of God, meet in the resurrection, of which all religion may be thought of as a pale shadow.[9]

Christianity forms links with religiosity through its central belief. But it also provides the critique of it through the one event which is the prerequisite of that resurrection, the crucifixion. 'The cross tests everything.'[10] It defies simple, permanent doctrinal categorizing and stands for self-criticism. God placards himself to be scrutinized, and those around the cross, both at Calvary and through the ages, by so examining this available God find salvation. The play of God's free choice goes hand in hand with the agony of his self-denial. Nothing can be given absolute, uncritical allegiance: all is to be tested.

In this context sacraments and common human experience may be considered together. Because the sacraments have become so significant for the church's life, they may at times become so much the church's possession that they almost cease to be of value. For example, in order to handle such potent symbols, the church has hedged them in with juridical questions: Who may preside? Who may participate? When and how may they be celebrated? The ultimate example is the concern with validity. But even this issue, which seems internal to the church, demonstrates how a sacrament of the resurrection, however much the church may claim it for itself, seems to be taken away from it by the critique which emanates from the cross. Article 26 of the Thirty-Nine Articles, for example, states that the unworthiness of the minister does not hinder the effect of the sacrament. Historically this can be argued. Bicknell neatly suggests that Judas' ministry might have been as effective as that of the other disciples.[11] But today, whatever theoretical justification for such a view may be devised, it will have little or no immediate pastoral value. People instinctively think of efficacy as an interactive idea. It might, for instance, be argued that any suitably qualified doctor may treat people effectively. But individuals exercise choice and go to the doctor whom they believe that they can know and trust. Such knowledge and trust are part of the condition for the cure. Similarly the effectiveness of the church's ministry is not determinable in terms of any theoretical legitimacy in the church. People recognize that limits are imposed on the minister's effectiveness by his believed worthiness. In other words, his ministry is not his possession, nor that of his church. It is a product of his interrelation with others.

If thinking about the sacraments and the occasional offices is brought into this frame of reference, we again find that what the church may presume to own and to offer to people, in fact already belongs to them. These sacraments are not the church's possession, but a facet of common human experience within God's creation, confirmed by the new creation in the resurrection. The church took over certain existing rituals and actions— water baptism, passover, and a shared meal. Other areas of life followed, notably marriage and death. It put itself in the way of people in such a way that the expression of life which the church endorsed in these sacraments was offered the specifically Christian test of the cross. Just as from time to time the resurrection has been used to obliterate the cross in Christian theology, so, for example, during Christendom, at times the alignment of what the church believed were its rites and what people held to be their human rituals has occurred. But the fact that this era is now over is not a reason for abandoning the significance which the gospel and the church have given to common human experience. Indeed it is impossible for the church to withdraw these rituals. In spite of the contemporary historical and liturgical narcissism that afflicts the church, they still do not belong to the church. If Christian ministers believe that they have to distance themselves and the church from the world in order to further mission and ministry, it is unlikely that any pulling back at this point will be seen as reasonable. It will be felt as an affront to human experience, which can never belong solely to the church. The anger which will be generated, which may take the form not just of aggression but also of apathy, will inhibit almost every wish that the church may have to proclaim its gospel.

This issue is not merely pragmatic or strategic, to be tested by counting or measuring responses to the gospel in the light of different pastoral approaches. It is concerned with the theological and pastoral valuation of human life. If, therefore, the church does withdraw from this work, it will not merely affect the people among whom it ministers. It will also diminish its own grasp of the gospel. Each time, for example, a baptism is performed, there is also a message to the church. Living in such interaction and with its attendant pains, the church is reminded that the claims of the gospel cannot be reduced to moral exhortations or subjective appeals. The 'something more', which is the mark of any theology of the grace of God, is implicit in the interaction between church and people in this rite. It may be that one 'something more' in a pluralist society might be to resist the pressures from many quarters to reductionism. This tries to make human life, which is divinely created as rich and multi-faceted, manageable within its own terms. The churches need a vision for the occasional offices which is like that of the writer to the Ephesians, from whom this term 'multi-faceted' is taken. He uses it to describe God's wisdom. The church's ministry surpasses all human comprehension. It is to make to God's wisdom known to the powers in heaven. Whether these are angels or demons does not matter here. The fascinating point is that in the only text in the New Testament which is explicit about what the church is for, we are shifted from all that is familiar, that can be known or can be tested, into the realm of the mysterious and unknown. This alone is a salutary warning to churches which become over-confident in knowing what they are for and who belongs.

To draw together this discussion of sacraments, rites and Christian theology, five points may be listed to inform theological thinking and pastoral practice.

1. Sacraments, which are inevitably linked with the occasional offices, are not specifically a Christian phenomenon. The Christian sacraments are to be understood and interpreted against this larger context and not *vice versa*. This is increasingly an insight shared by Protestant and Catholic thinkers alike, but it is not yet a basic presupposition with which ministers work.[12]

2. Sacraments are multi-faceted and not reducible to any one interpretation. When the Christian church was first forging its way, bishops and pastors were the theologians. The risk-taking in theology provided a means of interpreting everyday life and experience in such a way that the gospel commended itself for its realism. The theology of the sacraments today is also likely to develop among those engaged in a pastoral ministry. It will not be a secure point on to which they may fall back in the face of pastoral complexities.

3. There are three ways of viewing sacraments, which are not mutually exclusive. These are worth holding in mind as quick tests for interpreting the minister's experience as he ministers through the occasional offices: they provide a meaning for what is the case; they create something new and different; and they always refer to something other than what is immediately given. They are thus always in their richness connected with signs, symbols and life, making links between all three.

4. Sacraments have been called 'the doors to the sacred'. This description, if held in the context of a theology of the resurrection as new creation and the cross as the testing point for that celebration, reminds us that the sacred is not defined either as the church or by the church.

5. If the sacraments are so regarded, we may also see that they function on the working boundary of the church in order to preserve the church from itself. The social values that they reflect may be a better indicator at times of God's will than any ecclesiastical presumptions about them.

Notes

1. A. G. Herbert, *Liturgy and Society* (London, Faber, 1935), pp. 207ff. The ARCIC and Lima documents make similar assumptions.
2. D. Power, 'Editorial', *Concilium* 112 (1979), p. vii.
3. J. Martos, *Doors to the Sacred* (London, SCM, 1981), p. 163ff.
4. See J. D. C. Fisher, *Christian Initiation: Some Early Reformed Rites of Baptism and Confirmation* (London, SPCK, 1970).
5. See, e.g., R. Bocock, *Ritual in Industrial Society* (London, Allen & Unwin, 1974).
6. North, *Secular Priests*, p. 291.
7. Kavanagh, 'Life cycle', p. 17, quoting Robert Taft.
8. Among the descriptions listed by D. Boroborio, 'The "Four Sacraments" of popular religiosity. A critique', *Concilium* 112 (1979), pp. 85ff, are *rites de passage*; the catholicism of critical moments; festive catholicism; sacramental popular religiosity; cultural religion of life-cycles; the catholicism of the four seasons of life.
9. See Carr, *Pastor as Theologian*, pp. 202ff.
10. See Carr, *Tested by the Cross*. The remark is Luther's. See W. van Loewenich, *Luther's Theology of the Cross* (ET Belfast, Christian Journals, 1976).
11. E. J. Bicknell, *A Theological Introduction to the Thirty-Nine Articles of the Church of England* (London, Longmans, 1919), p. 462.
12. G. C. Berkouwer, *The Sacraments* (ET Grand Rapids, Eerdmans, 1969). Paul Tillich pointed out the dangers of 'pansacramentalism' which might follow such agreement. See *The Protestant Era* (ET London, SCM, 1951), pp. 105ff.

PART TWO

Ministering Through the Occasional Offices

Introduction

In this section of the book we shall examine the three main occasional offices—baptisms, weddings, and funerals. The focus turns now to the practical issues which they raise for the minister and his ministry. This is not to imply that the theological questions are forgotten. They will be allowed to emerge from the discussion and will not, therefore, be given the prominence of starting positions. The reason for this is that every minister, however she thinks about these matters and however confused she may be by them, has finally to make a judgement about what she is to do. I have proposed that there is theological justification for the church's deliberately remaining involved with people's experience at these points in life. That now constitutes the basis upon which this exploration of pastoral practice is developed.

Each chapter takes the same shape. After considering some of the background questions to each office, we shall explore how it might be handled. So far as possible, each step is illustrated with examples.

For clarity the ministry through each office has been described in terms of a simple system. The practice of ministry has four phases: approach, exploration, ritual and feedback. For the minister this process is informed and undergirded by a dominant mode. This indicates the area of reflection that is most involved. There are three such modes: religion, theology and practice. They do not precisely coincide with the process. 'Religion' refers to the way in which the church and minister are initially used as the focus for religious expression. The exploration and ritual phases are where ministers are expected to be specifically Christian, and so to employ their faith and belief. The move from ritual to feedback is where ministers learn from their involvement in this ministry and develop their theology as a whole.

Inevitably there are caveats. We are dealing with people and social behaviour. It is, therefore, impossible to lay down rules. In addition each parish and church will vary and so create different conditions for this ministry. So these chapters are not, and could not be, blueprints. They do, however, point to factors which any minister ought at least to note and consider. The illustrations have been drawn from actual instances of ministry, but there is no implication of case study. The aim is to offer a framework to assist pastors to interpret their everyday ministry through what they are being invited to do in the occasional offices.

SIX

Infant Baptism

For centuries most Christian churches have baptized or christened children. Those which have not have usually produced their own ceremony of dedication. The clergy of the Church of England have been required actively to encourage parents to have their new-born offspring baptized.[1] Such behaviour has not been without its critics inside, as much as outside, that church. The nineteenth century saw a major pastoral and theological upheaval over the issue. Not only were there disputes between church parties about baptismal regeneration, which consolidated around the Gorham case, but several parish clergy began to feel increasingly uncomfortable with the rite.[2] Hensley Henson, when Vicar of Barking, used a University Sermon at Oxford in 1896 to condemn the modern practice as 'indecent in itself, discreditable to the Church, and highly injurious to religion'. In 1907 Roland Allen resigned as Vicar of Chalfont St Peter on the grounds of the lack of differentiation between members of the church as believers with obligations and those who felt that they had a right to belong.[3] Neither Henson nor Allen were party men and each parish was socially different. After the Second World War similar views became more widespread among the clergy. Following debate at the Lambeth Conference (1948) and meetings of the Convocations (1942–54), an outline baptismal discipline was published in 1957.[4] But the clergy, both those who tried to observe it and those who did not, began to find that it led to conflict with their parishioners. As a result there were a number of conferences, such as the national ecumenical gathering promoted by Parish and People in 1965 and a series of diocesan events.[5]

In 1963 the Diocese of Chelmsford conducted a major study into baptism of infants. The clergy were uncomfortable and asked the bishop to promulgate a policy. After a

65

synod on the theology of baptism, clergy and lay synods discussed the issue. In 1967 over 1000 people (clergy and laity) voted on a series of propositions. That Holy Baptism is rightly administered to children was agreed by 94%. Preparation was expected by 98%, and 89% reckoned that the service should take place in the presence of a congregation of regular worshippers. They were more divided on the service of Thanksgiving for and Blessing of a Child. Nearly one third thought that it should be offered to all, including those looking forward to baptism.

In 1984 two researchers considered similar issues in the Diocese of Durham. They surveyed 800 lay people. Of these, 95% were in favour of infant baptism in principle and 75% believed that it should be offered to all. Overall non-parents tended to be more rigorous than parents, and younger church members more rigorous than older members. The survey was tied up with the question of the admission of infants to Holy Communion, but the result is not unlike that found in Chelmsford nearly twenty years previously.[6]

The main point that both studies brought out was the difference in attitude between clergy and laity. Generally it appears that infant baptism is regarded more highly by the laity as an opportunity for the church to meet people at a crucial moment in their lives. Ministers, by contrast, probably because they in the end take the service, feel the difficulties more acutely. In particular, however, this difference of attitude reminds pastors that the folk religion which they so often despise in those who seek the ministry of an occasional office is as potent within their congregations as outside.

In recent years the churches have given close attention to the doctrine and practice of baptism. The publication of *Baptism, Eucharist and Ministry* (the Lima Document) by the World Council of Churches tended to question the propriety of infant baptism. It concluded, however, with the notion of 'equivalent alternatives', thus allowing all the participating churches to remain together. In Great Britain the issue of baptism remains on the agenda of most churches.[7] The consensus, largely developed from the upsurge of liturgical studies, is that adult baptism is the norm, from which infant baptism derives. This is expressed in service books by putting the orders of service in that sequence.

In spite, however, of all this activity, for many ministers (with the obvious exception of Baptists) the issue of infant baptism is less clear. Church documents write with confidence about the children of believing parents or church members. Pastors, however, know that such definitions are not so easy in real life. What the minister may expect of someone claiming to be 'believing' may be very different from what that person understands. The Church of England because of its historical ministry finds itself in a particularly exposed position. This was well demonstrated in the debate in the General Synod in 1991.

From this ferment, however, a number of points consistently emerge. First, many ministers are still willing to baptize infants. But the churches are providing some protection of their consciences by allowing them to postpone the service or offer a blessing or thanksgiving in its place. What may be overlooked, however, is that this demands correspondingly greater sophistication of the applicants. They are required to, as it were, determine their degree of faith and so draw a distinction between baptism and blessing. Second, the congregation is being more involved in the rite, so that baptism is less a private affair. Even when the service is not held at the time of normal worship, members of the congregation are now often present. They are also increasingly involved in the preparatory work with parents. Third, in the Church of England and some others there is now agreement that if a baptism is requested of a minister other than the incumbent of the parish, there will be liaison between the ministers. This prevents people shopping around. But, fourth, probably the most significant change is that nearly one hundred percent today support some form of preparation. The Convocations of the Church of England addressed this topic in 1957. In spite of the demands on time and energy, both ordained and lay people believed that this was a point of ministry at which intensive work should be attempted. Today most baptisms are performed after preparation of some kind.

But if baptism now appears in this light to the church, it looks very different to those who seek it. Underlying the belief that infant baptism is possible is the church's assumption that adult baptism is the norm from which it derives. This is emphasized in the modern liturgies.[8] The church thus begins with an assumption about itself and about baptism as its rite. By contrast, however, for most people baptism is a rite which is performed on children, especially babies. Children themselves regard it as something done to babies, which is certainly not for them. The old word 'christening' persists, in spite of the church's attempts to replace it with its own term 'baptism'. Discussions in the churches generalize about the rite and the sacrament. But in the pastoral context the striking point, as with the occasional offices in general, is that each baptism is unique. The request itself often has its own surprising rationale, which is not explained away in terms of family customs or grandparental influence. For example, in urban and suburban parishes some ministers have observed a move away from family custom. Young parents seem to wish to express something about themselves and their new family, rather than merely to continue a tradition. Increased mobility disperses families. One result is that children may be presented for baptism a little later in life. The parents may have had to move away from their home area into new accommodation as soon as the child was imminent or born. By the time the second baby arrives they have settled into their new environment. They then bring both children as a token of their family having been established. This sort of observation has to be taken into account, if the minister and the applicant are to engage each other.

Since the request for baptism is peculiar to each person, the first and primary skill of the minister is that of listening carefully and hearing the coded phrases which give the clue to the point of contact. Some of these may be too quickly discounted. That a child can only inherit if baptized is obviously untrue. But the issue being raised by such a misapprehension may be that of the child's legitimate membership of family and society, when the parents are unsure of their own place within both. Another common assumption is that an unbaptized person cannot be buried in a churchyard. And regularly put forward is the proposition that the parents wish their child eventually to be married in church. It is easy for the minister to say that none of these has anything to do with baptism, although he might recall how often the church does enquire on its forms. But each of these apparently irrelevant questions contains clues. If, for example, baptism is thought of as concerned with the beginning of life, then marriage and burial seem distant. Each of these enquiries is about the role of parents. What may it mean to do the best for their child? How they can create the new continuity of the new family? This may be especially acute at the birth of the first child, but any subsequent child also disturbs the pattern of life. Then people are thrown up against their fundamental beliefs, hopes and fears. One increasingly common instance of this is reported by ministers. This is the divorced parent, usually the mother, who wishes through this rite to state to the child and to the world, as well as to herself, that divorce does not represent failure as a human being and unworthiness in society. Behind this and similar requests may lie the wish for the assurance that the child will have benefits in life which may have been denied to the parents.

We are now far from the discussion about the theology and practice of baptism. At times it seems that the gap between it and these pastoral issues cannot be bridged. One thing is sure. If for centuries the church has insisted on the baptism of infants, actively pursued parents to have it done, and urged it as a duty to God and to the child, it is not possible to reverse that teaching by a mere change of doctrinal stance. Ministers, therefore, need to be able to hear what people are requesting, and in order to do that they need to avoid pressures to categorize applicants. Clergy sometimes appear contemptuous of folk religion, with its simplistic beliefs. What people hold dear is dismissed as superstition. Little or no attempt is made to understand this pastorally or to interpret it theologically. But the problem facing ministers today is not unlike that facing St Paul in Athens. There he found the people 'god-fearing' or 'religiously scrupulous', not, as sometimes translated, 'superstitious' (Acts 17.22). He used the word as a sort of compliment and from that base interpreted the Athenians' religious beliefs in the light of the Christian gospel. How, then, are ministers to value human beliefs and feelings, both in the sense of acknowledging their integrity and, more intriguingly, perceiving their status within creation? That the outcome of this ministry will in every case be incomplete must follow from the uniqueness of every human encounter. But such incompleteness, although it may be discomforting, does not invalidate the

attempt. Eric James elucidated this in his reflections on
the 1965 conference, *Crisis for Baptism*. He describes how
a woman from a hostel for the homeless asked for her
baby to be baptized. She had no husband and no friends,
and the child had little, if any, obvious chance of being
brought up in a Christian environment. Nevertheless Eric
James involved some of the congregation and performed
the ceremony. In so doing, he argues, the congregation
and this lonely woman were reminded that they belonged
to each other under God, and she was assured that her
homeless, fatherless child was as valuable to God as any
other.

> To me the sacrament was that day proclaiming something
> new to the heart of the Gospel. I do not say that it is *the*
> Gospel. I do not say it is all of the truth of baptism; but it
> is part of the truth of baptism I am reluctant to surrender.[9]

The Approach

The range of possible reasons for coming to the church
seeking baptism for a child is as great as the style with
which the approach may be made. The type of parish or
church will affect this, as will the relationship, real or presumed, of the parents to the church. The rural vicar, with
the occasional baptism of a child about whose birth most,
if not all, will be aware, is in a different position from the
minister on a housing estate full of young parents and many
babies. The first may initiate the contact, whereas the latter
has no such opportunity. However, three principles underly
all such encounters. First, they are personal, and are concerned with a significant event in the parents' lives. It
may not be an important event—the child may not even
be wanted—but it is significant. The birth may not be a
joyous event, but the parent or parents often come. In
one large parish, where 300 or so children are baptized
each year, the vicar estimated that at least one third of
these baptisms dealt with a guilty secret. The child was
illegitimate or unwanted or abused. There was little joy
surrounding its birth or celebration over its baptism. But
the request was made. The encounter with the church is
significant and, since it is a personal encounter, care has
to be taken to ensure that it is felt to be just that. Second,
although the applicants may believe, and even feel, that

they are individuals, they also represent wider groupings than themselves and their immediate families. They will be largely unaware of this, except in so far as friends and acquaintances may be involved. But because they are also representatives within the larger society, the baptism is not, nor can it be, a private affair. Even a royal christening, which is sometimes criticized for being held in private, is not. Press coverage and publicity surround the event and few can fail to be aware that it is happening. Thirdly, unless they are regular worshippers, the parents are likely to be ignorant of the ethos, language and rituals of the church and to feel guilty about that ignorance. Their approach, therefore, will be nervous. Some may express this as bluster and demand, especially when faced with any scheme of preparation. Others will be diffident. The arrival of a single person to enquire about baptism is always interesting. Is he or she a single parent? Or does the appearance of one, usually the mother, evidence nervousness on the part of the couple? There is no way of knowing without careful attention and interpretation.

Every encounter has to be managed with these characteristics in mind. Certain practical consequences follow. First, no such approach can be treated casually. One way to emphasize the significance of any meeting is to manage it carefully. The urban vicar, therefore, who has a reliable system of being available for such requests at specific times at a particular place, conveys a message of willingness which is clearer than that of one who claims to be available at any time, but who either is not there when someone calls or appears upset by an intrusion at an awkward moment. The word used to describe such managed availability is not unimportant. Ministers frequently advertise a 'surgery', which offers a false analogy for what they are doing. It suggests the diagnostic stance of the doctor, which is inappropriate to the church's intentions and the applicants' expectations. Occasionally clergy complain that people seem to think that baptism is merely another service provided by the National Health Service. It may not be surprising that people think like this, when clergy go to such lengths to emulate it.

Many ministers use literature or videos during this approach phase. Whether locally produced or coming from one of the national societies or publishers, handouts are given titles like 'The Meaning of Baptism' or, more chattily, 'So You Want Your Child Baptised!'. One assumption that lies behind the provision of such material is that people can and do read it. But even if they are read, these leaflets underestimate the third aspect listed above—guilty ignorance. Few can understand or be expected to grasp a particular theology of baptism. Not many easily or naturally read anything at all. It may be useful to recall that even the Ethiopian eunuch, one of the few readers mentioned in the New Testament, could only manage an interesting but unfamiliar text with the aid of an interpreter (Acts 8.26ff). It is also apposite to note that, whereas many ministers complain that they lack time to read and study or that they find many books beyond them, they persist in laying this demand on others. There is a suspicion that the amount of literature or other visual material has increased in proportion to the discomfort felt about baptism on the part of ministers. It may, therefore, be not just an aid to ministry, but a defence against the minister's felt vulnerability. This is not a matter of social class—books for the literate, videos for others. Whoever approaches the church for a baptism of their child is expressing human feelings. These may be articulated and require one response; they may be haltingly unclear and demand a different one. The key point for all is that the expectation is that meeting should be personal enough for people to feel that their own emotions are recognized. The belief is that the minister embodies in him or herself a human presence of the divine, which can be encountered. A hand-out of leaflet, tape or video, therefore, will not suffice.

There is one exception. Since most applicants are likely to be nervous, a written reminder of a meeting, together with some description of its purpose and what might happen at it, and, maybe, the details required for the register should be offered. These, when given in the setting of a personal meeting constitute an enabling invitation to continue the personal encounter established through the initial contact.

To whom is the approach made? This is a different question from how the church can manage the first encounter. The churches today have all in their various fashions endorsed the idea of lay ministry. Such ministry as working with those seeking baptism for their children is no longer automatically assumed to be a professional responsibility. There is undoubtedly value in this. Such arrangements, however, may be inadvertently set up for the benefit of the church rather than as a ministry with the applicants. We need, therefore, always to consider their perspective before launching into a theoretical ministry.

People seeking baptism arrive with a complex set of notions. Some have already been mentioned. Underlying all, however, is the generalized idea of 'God' or 'the church'. It is a mark of human experience that such massive notions are likely to be most effectively addressed if they can be in a sense located. Since they represent an awesome dimension to life, with which in the nature of the case the applicants only rarely become involved, part of the belief system is that authorized ministers are those who are best qualified to manage them. It is a mark of dependence that people construct in their minds a hierarchy of competence and authority. Thus while the churches are seeking with good reason to diminish such notions in terms of their ministries, the working reality is that people come with such a structure in their minds. The minister as 'God-person', one who can confidently be relied upon to handle the boundaries of birth, life and death, is not a theme in many contemporary theories of ministry. But it is a key component in ministering with many people, including most of those who bring their children for baptism. A publicly authorized minister, therefore, is needed in this approach phase.

In some places the minister will be the natural person initially to handle the meeting. In other places, especially where the occasional offices are a major demand on time and energy, the negotiation may be delegated to a secretary or lay volunteer. Such delegation, however, needs careful preparation, not only so that the person or persons concerned know what they are doing, but even more so that they understand the nature of their authority in the light of people's expectation.[10]

For the applicant, therefore, a key sense is that of looking for a recognizably church person. This may be different from the keenest Christian member of a church. For someone is sought who can be believed to possess an adequate authority to represent that church (or God) in the mind, with which the applicant arrives. Ministers, therefore, have a task to perform at a stage well before that in which they become embroiled in questions of theology, rite and preparation.

The aim of this approach phase is to begin the process of engagement between the applicant and the church. The chief requirement is a sense of reliability and dependability, so that the hesitations and uncertainties, which all concerned have, may be explored and interpreted in the light of the gospel. How such reliability is created will vary from context to context. But however it is attempted, it cannot be casually achieved. It requires reflection and forethought. For example, when a person enquires about baptism, a minister may warmly respond that he will call. This seems to him a friendly and reassuring stance. But even so simple an act needs thought. In that locality, for example, who calls? In many areas a home visit implies a threat—police, rent collector, social worker, Jehovah's Witness. The prevailing idea is of someone who arrives with demand, however legitimate. In other places to call is to presume upon a relationship which has yet to be established, while in others it is a socially acceptable form of behaviour arranged through the diary. A sensitive minister will be alive to such local attitudes and devise an appropriate response. It is often important that there should be a visit, but usually not as the first encounter with the applicants. There is a seriousness about the call for them, which shows in the care with which preparations are made. But underlying all is a residual anxiety that it would somehow be wrong for the vicar to discover them as they actually are. Even in so small a matter ministry shows itself to be something shared with people, not done to them.

However the meeting is arranged, the aim remains consistent in every circumstance—to lead people from their present position to a clearer understanding of what they are requesting. The process itself constitutes reassurance and care, and is best described as a negotiation. This rather cold word has the merit of directing attention to the parties in the meeting. The minister may not presume immediate intimacy, even though the dependency in the situation might encourage him to feel (wrongly) that he can. The applicants are assured that their ignorance is properly theirs and is not dismissed or prejudged. The negotiation is about establishing the expectations of the parents; what the possibilities are of their being realized; and whose responsibility this will be. It is a thoroughly human negotiation, in that it persistently returns to the basic stance that they are the parents and they are, therefore, responsible under God for the life of their child, whatever they may ultimately decide. It is also, therefore, important that this encounter, wherever and however it is arranged, should involve the baby itself. He or she has a legitimate interest, however small, and without this physical presence both applicants and minister may unwittingly slide into unreal areas in the negotiation.

The approach phase of the process has limited aims and one task. The task is to enable applicants and the church to establish working boundaries. This term is used not to refer to barriers of membership, who is in and who is out, nor to issues of the parents' standing in relation to the church. 'Boundary' is a notional way of describing that which between the applicants and the minister has to be neither assumed nor ignored but carefully and deliberately worked on.[11] The aims of the church are to establish this through a considerate welcome, which assures the parents that whatever they may dimly want or feel is valued for its own sake. How such boundaries are established and negotiated will affect the total ministry of the church. The mother of a new-born child is a member of one of the greatest freemasonries— mothers with prams. Any inconsistency on the part of the minister is instantly picked up and widely broadcast. To propound a public policy, therefore, as if baptisms were a kind of political manoeuvre by the church and to fail to manage the parents' approach, will leave many unhappy legacies.

Exploring the Meaning

But what if the number of those approaching is overwhelming? Even with a joint lay and clergy ministry, it is possible for a church to be overwhelmed by numbers. One of the advantages of thinking about such ministry in a systematic fashion is that it allows the same task to be performed but using different methods according to the demands of the context and the resource available. In one large Church of England parish the numbers enquiring about baptism were running at between 15 and 30 per week. The vicar and his colleagues could have spent all their time on this ministry. That was out of the question, even though all, lay and ordained, were strongly committed to using this encounter as a positive point of the ministry of the gospel. While church-going in this urban setting was not high, association through the occasional offices remained strong.

The solution devised was elegant. The vicar advertized that requests for baptism would be discussed at the church on Wednesday nights. The ministers and the congregation mobilized themselves for this work. There was always one ordained minister present throughout the evening. But the bulk of the ministry was done by lay people. Those enquiring about baptism were encouraged to come together, to bring the baby and any friends or relations they wished. The wider involvement in the baptism was recognized from the outset. They were welcomed in the church hall, where tea and coffee were offered. Members of the congregation mingled with the applicants. Care was taken to ensure that a large proportion of these were parents themselves. A lot of informal help was offered to young mothers and personal contacts were made. In another room trained lay people welcomed the parents and began a preliminary discussion about the request for baptism. They took details of names and addresses, any other contact with the church and outlined the preparation programme that the church offered. But—and this was most important—they also gave the families the date on which the baptism would take place, if they followed the programme. In so doing the church recognized that the baptism was more than the service. For family purposes plans had to be made for a certain date. Throughout the evening the minister was available to give advice or simply to meet people.

The evening did not end for the couple and their family when the details had been taken. It was announced and arranged as a full evening, and people knew what they had bargained for. At the end of the evening, everyone was invited into the church. There the minister welcomed them, gave an initial very brief talk on baptism and the preparation programme. Everyone then shared in the Service of Thanksgiving for the Birth of a Child from the Alternative Service Book. This brief service expressed a basic human feeling, and without exception people said how much they appreciated it. Subsequently one of the ministers of the parish called, as arranged, and talked about baptism, and people came on to the parish programme. Interestingly at that point a number of people withdrew their enquiry. In the welcome of the church and the service of thanksgiving they had found what they were seeking. Most importantly, they had done so on their terms, without feeling judged or having been offered a second best alternative to baptism.

Few ministers consider baptizing children without some attempt at prior meeting with the parents and, when possible, the godparents. This preparation may range from a quick glance at the order of service, with an optimistic attempt at explaining the content, to a demanding series of meetings. Some pastors insist on regular attendance at church over a period. What is remarkable, however, is the way in which many parents, in spite of such rigorous demands, often persist through to the baptismal rite, only to absent themselves until the next child is born.

This section of the chapter, however, is not entitled 'preparation', since that term has misleading implications. The prefix 'pre-' provides the clue: it refers to work done prior to the main operation. Food, for example, is prepared before it is cooked and eaten. At school 'prep' is done before the main business of lessons. If this picture is used in connection with baptism, the main operation becomes the performance of the rite itself. It is thus not surprising if people regard that as the climax of the process and feel that their part is now over. That is not the intention of preparation, but it may be an inadvertent effect. Similarly the term, if used publicly—'Come to the preparation classes'—has more immediate overtones of the ante-natal class, which has been the parents' most recent experience of such demand. That, too, is directed to a definite end—the successful birth of the baby. So, by extension, a baptism preparation class may be assumed to lead simply to a successful baptism. The church, by focusing on preparation, may raise false expectations both in the parents and among its own members, which are bound to conflict. The church's assumption is about life-long commitment, development and growth into adult membership. The applicants' view is different. They look for a one-off rite. The notion of preparation, therefore, is not helpful. An exploration of meaning is required, as these questions are raised in encounter between the parents and the church and its minister.

Only if the applicants have established a sense of relationship through the approach phase is exploration and interpretation possible. The task of this phase is to provide parents with an opportunity to discover the significance of their request. To some this may not sound sufficiently Christian or proclamatory. But this is where the skill of pastoral ministry lies. By their coming at all the applicants have expressed some sort of belief, however incoherent. It is the pastor's responsibility to relate that belief to the richness of the Christian gospel which he or she stands for, so that in those people's lives God may be discerned and responded to. The gospel is not something to be protected by its ministers; it is constantly being created as a new dynamic or power (Rom. 1.16).

If, as has been argued, the applicants' approach is concerned with the experience of parenthood, then the exploration also focuses on those issues. New parents are generally only too happy and pleased to be invited to talk about what it is to become a parent. There is little point in expositions of the gospel or the imposition of ecclesiastical customs in the hope that these might be grasped as alternative matters of significance. That can only reinforce the ignorant guilt of the parents and leave the observer again amazed at the amount of stress they will endure for the good of their child. The alternative to such a teaching stance, however, is very often today presented as collusion with the parents around romanticized views of love and parenthood, all of which is vindicated by the church's blessing.

Neither of these approaches to ministry is adequate. Pastoring always involves teaching. It is not possible to do one without the other. This congruence underlies the idea of the local minister as both pastor and teacher within his parish or area. If these two functions are held in tandem, they moderate each other. The notion of pastoring necessarily includes interpretation of what is being done and why: that of teaching is adjusted by the addition of pastoring, so that it cannot be merely reduced to the presentation of information, whether by lecture, discussion or leaflet. A quality of life as it is lived lies at the heart of teaching. The concept of interpretation is a clearer way of considering this activity. For such ministry the concept of a negotiated interpretation is the clearest way of thinking. It emphasizes the interaction between all concerned, not just at the personal level but also for what they represent. Thus, for instance, a child's parents (a new role) meet an ordained minister (a public role), as well as three people meet—the personal level. Theologically we may have representatives of the specific dimension of divine creativity (the parents) in conjunction with a representative of the richness of the idea of God (the minister). Negotiation, or collaboration, produces the gospel interpretation of these lives.[12]

Any exploration of the significance and meaning of parenthood requires such a negotiated interpretation. If the focus is on parenthood, a teaching approach, for example, might leap directly to ideas of God's fatherhood and Christ's sonship, using a Pauline model. But this deprives the parents of the one thing which is the reason for their present contact with the church. It is *their* parenthood, not God's, that is at stake. An alternative, therefore, might be to range over the experiences of parenthood as these present themselves. This in itself is another reason for having the baby somewhere nearby. Familiar thoughts include creation—the new life is a source of wonder; or love and self-giving—the cost of having the child often emerges both in terms of limitations on the parents' freedom and their relationship. Negative feelings also arise, not least with those who may be unmarried or abused and others with secrets about which they feel too guilty to speak. Facing such issues is likely to lead the parents and the pastor to one of the fundamental questions before both: is baptism a contract or a covenant?

The difference between contract and covenant is argued by most ministers in the course of their theological studies. But when it emerges in the type of exploration that is here being described, it may be seen also as an importantly human issue. A popular belief is that in this world you only get what you pay for. Nothing is free. When enquiring about a baptism, parents bring with them this ineradicable belief that contractual behaviour is the norm. Everything has its *quid pro quo*. If the parents do something, then God for his part will respond by playing his role. The church often colludes with this diminishing view of God, in spite of such warnings as that of F. D. Maurice:

> If you make your faith and your responsibility the conditions of God's covenant, and not God's covenant the warrant for your faith and your responsibility, I am greatly afraid that you will soon believe only in yourselves.[13]

But the one thing that is in fact most obviously absent from the newly formed relationship between parent and baby is a contract. There is, and can be, no established *quid pro quo*: the love, affection and upbringing of the child, whatever the emotional gratification, are necessarily free acts of covenantal love. This has important consequences for the exploration phase of the process. Oliver Quick has pointed out that, while the marriage relationship is contractual, that between parent and child is qualitatively different. For it can have 'no beginning or end except the beginning or end of the child's existence'.[14]

The idea of covenant, therefore, does not spring from specifically Christian views of God. It is implicit in the new relationship, which is the reason for the encounter between parents and minister. It cannot be introduced by the minister as a theological imposition upon some neutrally valued relationship, since it is the material for the exploration of the significance of the parents' request, which is provided by the parents themselves. This may be interpreted with the assistance of the minister, whose own frame of reference is ordered and informed by the Christian gospel. Clergy sometimes express disappointment at the apparent lack of response to their efforts to proclaim the covenantal love of God. But this derives from their failure to grasp the nature of the covenant with which they are dealing and which they are being invited, as a privilege, to help the parents explore.

This exploration, therefore, is conducted by the applicants. This implies that it may venture into areas which the minister finds uncharted. His tendency may be to create an all-embracing structured course or series of sessions (of which he determines the number) into which parents slot. The assembly-line image may not be lost on them. The effect is unfortunate. Coming with a vague sense of responsibility for the child and for this new life, the parents are in danger of being unburdened of their glimmer of significance as soon as they arrive. But if the work of ministry is to match the interpretation that has been outlined, the corollary is that the parents manage any meeting, not the church or its ministers.

Locating control where it belongs is the first recognition of any act of ministry. A context is required in which they can be invited to assume the responsibility which is theirs, so as to create a means of expressing, exploring and evaluating their ideas and feelings. Ministries, therefore, help to create rather than impose a theological frame for interpreting human life especially their own. For the minister this is a dangerous and often threatening exercise. He may be confronted with areas of ignorance in himself; he may find theological ideas being developed which he had hitherto thought heretical or had never even conceived; and all demand that he responds. He may do this by emphasizing a particular view of baptism. But if so pressed, the minister might usefully recall the earlier review of what baptism has been at various times in history. It may be that a theology of baptism for a particular time and place has to be developed through the exploration carried out by parents with the local theologian, the minister. The theology of the sacraments will be enlarged as a result of this genuine engagement between the church and the applicants for baptism. Discoveries about God for both parties are implied by such an understanding.

The Rite

Part of this exploration is introducing and examining the rite itself. There is today a tendency to reduce rites to rituals. Frank Wright has pointed out that ministers seem to respond well to invitations to study liturgy and its performance more than almost any other facet of their ministry. He wryly comments that the priest and Levite in the story of the Good Samaritan may well have been on their way to a liturgical conference to judge by the way they avoided pastoral matters in their haste.[15] It is easy to substitute a concern for getting the liturgy right for the rite itself. Clergy have been preoccupied with how forms of service may best be performed rather than with creating, together with the parents, suitable forms of expression for what they wish to say. In so doing the religious process of the rite may inadvertently be isolated from the underlying presence of the grace of God, for which the Christian gospel stands. Examples of this may be observed in two recent instances—the creation of alternative rites to that of baptism and the introduction of new forms of service.

Whatever the rationale behind the production of a Service of Thanksgiving and Blessing (and even more confusedly one of Naming and Blessing), it is noteworthy that this is the one occasional office for which alternative rituals are now offered. There is not yet a two-tier office for marriage (although some are beginning to advocate it over the question of the marriage of divorcees) or for funerals. A study of a number of parishes and their policies suggests that the deliberate choice of such a service instead of baptism is more likely to be that of committed Christians than of the casual applicant. The ceremony of Thanksgiving has the trappings of baptism, except for the water and the godparents. The service is held in church; the child is held by the minister; the name is often given; and a candle may be presented to the parents. The main difference, however, is that such a service is for the parents, while baptism is for the child. Indeed, Thanksgiving and Blessing may better be regarded as a replacement for the now dated ceremony of Churching, which persists only in few localities. As such its use as part of the exploration of meaning through baptism can be valuable. As a substitute for baptism, however, it chiefly functions to salve the minister's conscience. Once again, therefore, we are face to face with the perennial question of all Christian ministry: who bears the cost of painful moments and difficult experiences?

Liturgical scholarship is one of the most ecumenical of disciplines. As a result the changes in orders of service which have happened in many churches are remarkably similar.[16] But they are also created by people who believe that content matters more than anything else. But this is not the case in worship. Content is important, but not everything. This is especially true of liturgies for the occasional offices. For those with a slight connection with the church, all language is likely to be foreign. Even for regular worshippers the material in these offices is, in the nature of the case, going to be unfamiliar. The basic faults of new liturgies, which are exposed if they are used as the basis for engagement with applicants, are two. First, there is persistent assertion—'We are', 'We do'. For rituals which are to handle people's emotions, which are confused and today possibly even more so than hitherto, there are insufficient tentative expressions to be used as access points to the process of worship. This leads to either too much self-awareness and examination, thus not encouraging people to be carried by the ritual, or to none at all. The second weakness lies in the wish to say everything and, therefore, too much. For example, in the new rite for infant baptism in the Alternative Service Book, the service begins with a long introduction, which requires knowledge of salvation history. At the time of baptism there is an excluding emphasis upon the alternative family. In the opening there is mention of the church as a family, and the image becomes contentiously explicit when a child is old enough to understand it. In Section 43 the child is told that through baptism it becomes part of 'a new family'. Apart from the dubious theological justification for this description of the church, it seems curious at the moment when the family of the parents and child is being experienced intensely, as they gather with their friends and supporters, to introduce the child to an alternative, and by implication competitive, family, which most will have difficulty in comprehending.[17] The one major problem, however, to which many working pastors return in their efforts to make this ministry a genuine interpretation of people's lives and a proclamation of the gospel, is the lack of joy in the worship. There is worthy wordiness and laborious explanation. But little or no acknowledgement that for the families this may be a joyful moment. Since, at least in the Anglican liturgy, there is little room for extemporization, the problem is acute. It might be wise to use the first three sections of the Thanksgiving for the Birth of a Child before embark-

ing on the baptism service. Other small points of freedom
are the hymns. Lastly, the welcome could be elaborated,
although this comes rather late in the service. One other
thought might be to take the Signing with the Cross at
the earlier point in the service and make something of it.
In that way amid the rather church-preoccupied liturgy,
the experiences of the families can be acknowledged.

Holding to the distinction between rite and ritual is
one way of enabling the minister to exercise a ministry in
these circumstances. The ritual may be thought of as providing the boundaries and means by which it is possible
to participate in the rite. As such, therefore, ritual is
expected to have its own idiom and style, which may not
become ends in themselves. To engage with people in the
ways that have been outlined implies careful use of the
available rituals. These follow a prescribed form, and it is
not open to the minister to develop a form which allows
the parents to express what they wish alone. The rite is a
public event and its ritual expression is one factor in
keeping it so. It emphasizes the reality of the boundary
between church and applicant and the negotiation which
is necessary. The form of service, however, can be opened
up as part of the exploration of meaning. If the things,
which the parents discover that they wish to express,
emerge in the course of this exploration, they can be
gathered together and set alongside the order of service
to see where this expresses them adequately, where it
seems not to, and, most importantly, where it brings
from the resources of the church's gospel and history
ideas and interpretations which the parents may not possess. In the course of this activity it may be appropriate
for the minister to respond to requests for something
other than baptism, as these emerge from the discussion.
But eagerly to offer an alternative is an escape from the
work and demands of ministry. This is not a mechanical
activity. It requires skilled teaching of the sort which
comprises the heart of pastoral ministry.

The service is part of the total process that is being
described and not an end in itself. The text may be used to
link the exploration of meaning to the rite itself, the ritual
of which is then an expression of that understanding. Some
of these issues will have been raised during the exploration by the applicants with the minister. But baptism is

a public act and a public service. This is a recently recovered emphasis.[18] There is, therefore, another component to the rite—the members of the church. They, too, need to understand their role, not merely so that they may appear competent at any service and thus serve the applicants' necessary dependency, but also so that the second aspect of the sacrament—its ministry to the church—may function. Although public baptism during the main service of the church's worship is widely advocated, this can be unreasonable in places, for example, where baptisms occur almost every Sunday. No congregation will develop its life in an atmosphere of continual baptisms. From the point of view of the ministry with the applicants, too, this arrangement is not always desirable. The modern eucharistic rites, with their congregation-centred emphasis and declaratory style, are not the most welcoming form of worship for the neophyte, even after explanation. Each church will have its conditions and develop its own way of coping, but all have to enquire about the task of this phase in the baptismal process.

The main service of the church may stand for the gathering of Christian people, or it may merely appear to be another, alternative ritual in which the applicants are required to participate. There are ways of expressing the involvement of the congregation in baptism without requiring this to be indicated through one particular form of liturgy. Indeed, it would appear to be an extraordinarily limited group of Christians that could only worship in one way. If the church insists on baptisms at, say, 9.30 a.m. on a Sunday morning, without taking into account mobility and family movement, it will not be surprising if its worship, far from being a boundary across which people can move to discover significance in life, will become a barrier to all but the most resilient. There is no reason to leave all this exploration to the parents. The Christian congregation may also be taught about the responsibilities and demands of the baptismal life-style, which they are authorized by their own baptism to exemplify. This includes sharing other people's experience at some expense to one's own time. For this to be effective, however, the task has clearly to be understood. Members of the congregation are not asked to be present; they are required to be partners with the minister in the carefully prepared process of baptism, particularly at the ritual phase. In this way the sacrament is liberated to serve parents and child, minister and congregation alike. There is no better example in practice of what the churches discuss so often in theory—collaborative ministry between ordained and lay. It is also, as Kuhrt points out, a further collaboration between the church and God and therefore requires intense attention.[19]

The baptismal rite is heavily loaded with symbols, which do not especially belong to the church. The minister's task in ordering the service cannot be performed if he merely indulges his predilections. He is acting on behalf of a range of people, using powerful symbols which he does not control. His own ministry in this field, therefore, requires constant scrutiny, both from the feed-back which comes from others and that which he finds in himself. For he will develop and adjust the ritual as he performs it over the years. Religious symbols are powerful, but from time to time they lose their potency. For example, among the symbols which at various times have been associated with Christian baptism, have been the sign of the cross, light, a white robe, immersion, anointing, breath, the dove, fire, light, and, of course, water (although even this apparently simple ingredient can prove more complicated than it sounds—hot or cold, running or still). Around each of these is a heap of associations, some natural and primitive and others conditioned by Christian culture. The minister may too easily be locked into the latter. For example, Michael Perham comments that baptism is '*most obviously* about healing and wholeness'.[20] This may or may not be true, but it is not obviously so. Today's trends to the repristinization of liturgical activity may, if not handled with care, divorce the minister from the material of the process of ministry in which he is engaged. All aspects of the ritual, therefore, need regular scrutiny.

A specific example may be taken from the giving of the lighted candle. To the Christian this may be a sign of the light of Christ, as the baptismal candle is lighted from the paschal candle, which itself is sited near the font. The whole ceremony is redolent with powerful symbolism, which has been endorsed by the Christian church. But some parents exhibit discomfort at receiving the candle, not knowing what to do with it, and finally extinguishing it. For them the light of life applies less to Christ than to the infant, and it is this new-born, precious life which appears to be snuffed out ceremonially. Instead of bringing people through dimly held beliefs into a glimpse of the light of the gospel, the casual use of this symbol may plunge them further back into superstition. It is also observable that this occurs as much with church members, who bring their children for baptism, as for anyone. The way for a minister to avoid such pitfalls and minister as effectively as he might in such circumstances is through careful reflection on his experience and, so far as he can, on what he sees of the applicants. He may then adjust the ritual, less in the light of new liturgical insights, useful as these sometimes prove, than as people appear to make use of the rich, multi-valent symbolism of the rite.

Feed-back

The final phase of the process is feed-back. This term is preferable to the more customary 'follow-up', since it reminds the minister that, whatever her contribution to the process, she is part of it. She does not control what happens.

It is unlikely that there will be very much direct feed-back from those whose children the minister baptizes. The mobility of people means that it is more probable that she will pick up responses to the ministry of others. She is, therefore, caught up both in a network of pastoral practice, of which she will be unaware in any detail, and of people's lives on which other ministers and churches have at various times impinged. This rather vague material, often communicated in feelings and unconscious behaviour, constitutes feed-back. A variety of approaches to local follow-up of baptismal contacts has been attempted: visiting, a cradle-roll, cards delivered by members of the church (often the Mothers' Union), attempts to link mothers with women's groups, street wardens, and invitations to anniversary services. Behind all these, however, remains the assumption that the baptism of the child was an event between the family and the church. But the parents represent more than this, and the church, too, is larger than its own self-awareness. Any one-to-one contact, therefore, will be loaded with other concerns of the church, much to the parents' mystification and to the despair of the church members. Such misunderstanding is not helpful to future pastoral work and at worst it may produce the sort of despair which typifies reports on such enterprises.

If, however, the focus of the whole process is seen to be the rite itself, then the feed-back will be more diverse and diffuse than the minister and his congregational colleagues might hope. It is also, therefore, less personally gratifying. This generic problem in ministry through the occasional offices is discussed below. Feed-back occurs through the normal pastoral ministry that continues, and the test of baptismal ministry will be the extent to which the model of ministry as interpretation is sustained and allowed in other contexts and through other opportunities. One priest remarked that it was almost uncanny how often his next contact with a family after a baptism was through the funeral of a grandparent of the child. The continuing ministry of the church will depend on the extent to which people, in however general a fashion, can discern coherent involvement and interpretation of their lives through fleeting contacts with the churches and their ministers.

Notes

1. The opening rubric of the Order for the Public Baptism of Infants in the Book of Common Prayer.
2. P. J. Jagger, *Clouded Witness: Initiation in the Church of England in the Mid-Victorian Period* (Pennsylvania, Pickhurst, 1982).
3. Hensley Henson cited in C. E. Pocknee, *Infant Baptism Yesterday and Today* (Oxford, Mowbray, 1966), p. 1; R. Allen, 'To the parishioners of Chalfont St Peter', in D. Paton and C. H. Long ed., *The Compulsion of the Spirit. A Roland Allen Reader* (Grand Rapids, Eerdmans, 1983), pp. 126ff.
4. *Holy Baptism, Confirmation and the Communicant Life* (London, SPCK, 1957).
5. B. Moss ed., *Crisis for Baptism* (London, SCM, 1965).
6. G. H. G. Hewitt, *A History of the Diocese of Chelmsford* (Chelmsford, Chelmsford DBF, 1984), pp. 179ff. J. Astley

and W. Pickering, 'Who cares about baptism?', *Theology* 89 (1986), pp. 264–268.

7. For a summary of positions see A. S. Yates, *Why Baptize Infants?* (Norwich, Canterbury Press, 1993).

8. P. J. Jagger, *Christian Initiation, 1552-1969* (London, SPCK, 1970).

9. Eric James, 'Reflections on the conference', in Moss, *Crisis*, p. 138.

10. Carr, *Priestlike Task*, pp. 53ff.

11. Miller and Rice, *Systems*, pp. 262ff.

12. Shapiro and Carr, *Lost in Familiar Places*, p. 5.

13. F. D. Maurice, *Prophets and Kings of the Old Testament* (London, Macmillan, 1870), p. 216.

14. O. C. Quick, *The Christian Sacraments*, p. 167.

15. F. Wright, *The Pastoral Nature of Ministry* (London, SCM, 1980), p. 4.

16. For a summary see Yates, *Why Baptize Infants?*, ch. 12.

17. E. de Waal, 'The changing Anglican attitude towards the family', *Crucible* (1982), pp. 106ff. C. A. Lewis, 'The idea of the Church in the parish communion', *Crucible* (1982), pp. 114f.

18. This was reinforced by rubric in the Church of England in 1662, but it has recently become a major issue. See Canon B12. Other churches have examined the issue, too.

19. Kuhrt, *Believing in Baptism*.

20. Perham, *Liturgy*, p. 7. My italics.

SEVEN

Weddings

———

Baptism proves complicated for the church, largely because of the mix of sacramental theology and a rite of common human experience. Weddings, however, bring problems for the reverse reason. Although some use the word 'sacrament' of marriage, few doubt that the couple themselves are the ministers and not the church or the clergy. But it does not follow from this that the couple contemplating marriage may do whatever they wish. Around marriage today there is a range of questions which are generated by changes both in society and in the understanding of its institutions, as well as in the psychological interpretation of persons. Books and reports abound. Marriage is problematic, however, primarily because of the way that social and personal changes coincide in it.[1]

Marriage is a social institution. The law has a deep and legitimate interest in it. The Christian connection is secondary to its being a human institution. Most customs, for example, are pre-Christian in origin—the ring, presents, groomsmen and bridesmaids, and much of the ceremonial that marks a modern wedding, whether in a church or a registry office.[2] Today's discussions and concerns about marriage and the family are implicitly about the nature of our society and its future. The question 'Whither marriage?' is less about the couple than about the sort of society that is envisaged, hoped for and being created. The wealth of sociological analysis, anthropological comparison and political intention that is generated around marriage finally issues in the couple as they sit with a minister discussing their wedding. Their apparently simple relationship—man and woman—is set within a maelstrom of profound uncertainty and unsureness. It is, therefore. to be expected that they will to some extent feel this in themselves, even if, as is most likely, they will not be able to articulate the feelings.

Marriage is today regarded as highly personal. The union of two people possesses almost more privacy in British society than the life of the individual. The notion of consent, as in 'consenting adults', has a wider impact than merely on homosexual activity. Marriage is losing its contractual dimension: that is being put in some cases into legally binding pre-marital settlements. As a result it becomes an intensely personal relationship. As that happens, however, the customary associations with marriage decline. Sexual behaviour, for instance, is decreasingly considered a distinctive part of marriage. Certainly children are a separate consideration. In the decade from 1981 to 1991 the number of live births outside marriage in the United Kingdom rose from one in eight to nearly one in three. Marriage also declined, although not so quickly. And even though one in three marriages ends in divorce, this does not mean that marriage itself is despised. In 1991 37% of all marriages were between two divorced people.

Marriage, therefore, remains popular, but it is not what the Christian church has recently considered it to be. A marriage is less sexual and more personal, and each partner holds higher expectations of personal satisfaction. These, however, are less definable than the traditional expectations in marriage. There is accordingly still a high investment in marriage, although whether this makes for a more or less stable institution remains debatable. Ministers need to be continually alert to these dimensions to marriage when they meet any couple. The churches formally have great and understandable difficulty in coming to terms with these changes.[3] But it is in the midst of such a world that the pastor operates.

Somewhere between the overarching social expectations of the institution of marriage and the inflated personal investment of the couple lies the reality of the two who wish to marry. But the pair, too, has to be conceived as more than the sum of the personal, familial or social expectations. It generates its own dynamic. In any social context or group the couple stands for considerable power and consequently is more of a threat than is sometimes recognized. A pair always stands for investment, both by the couple and others, in a hoped-for future. This is the case even with the most transitory of pairs, and is more so in any pair which publicly announces its intention of remaining together for a long period.[4] At the same time such a pair can also be destructive. 'Two's company; three's a crowd' is an accurate description of common experience, with its implication that the way in which a couple functions excludes others. In society such pairing is institutionalized in marriage, which therefore not surprisingly remains a highly regarded activity. Although there is a discernible trend towards weddings in Registry Offices, many marriages in England are still solemnized in church. The meaning of this is difficult to ascertain. This is partly because of regional variations and partly because of different attitudes in different churches and, in the case of the Church of England, between different incumbents within that church, to the marriage of divorcees. The presenting reasons for requesting a church wedding sometimes seem superficial—flowers, a nice building, a setting for photographs, and music. None of these issues is easy to deal with. But underlying them are deeper issues for the churches and their ministers.

Marriage is more than a social requirement. Cohabitation is more widely acceptable than it was. Over 20% of those who marry for the first time are living together, and 60% or more of those marrying for the second occasion have already lived with their partner. Personal relationships of profound intimacy are not confined to marriage. But this new-found tolerance is not acquired without corresponding public uncertainties, and it may be that the church is being used not to endorse one stance or the other on such issues, but to hold the two in uncomfortable tension, while people sort themselves out. The Church of England, for example, has made heavy weather over the marriage of divorcees. Reports, synodical debates, procedural disputes, episcopal dissociation, have all marked an argument that has continued for many years. The outcome is not yet settled fully. Although the battle is fought on grounds of Scripture and tradition, it seems more likely that one reason why the church cannot settle the matter is because, as a body involved with people at their most dependent and carrying the expectations of a confused society that there is an answer, it is in a position from which it will not be able to extricate itself. The church expresses this difficulty on behalf of society but uses its own language of compassion while supporting an ideal of marriage. Its error may be that it thinks this language actually circumscribes an issue which is more subtle than it cares to acknowledge. The topic has been discussed elsewhere.[5] Here it is mentioned as the background to pastoral practice. Yet 'background' itself is not a helpful concept in such an examination. What is in question is the context of this ministry. The minister and the couples will be working not against a background of these larger phenomena but with them, and specifically as these are found within the particular couple and their engagement with the church. The ministry through this occasional office, therefore, will be one contribution to the way church and society may struggle to whatever new understanding is applicable and desired.

The minister holds the larger social context of marriage as this focuses in each couple. There is also the contemporary expectation of marriage as a personal relationship, which can be reduced neither to an economic contract nor to permission for sexual activity. Such factors themselves emphasize that the key to the process is that the couple are the ministers of the sacrament and creators of the new entity. The church's ministry is concerned with human beings as human beings. The phrase 'Christian marriage' sometimes occurs. Those who are practising Christians might wish to consider the way in which the dimension of their joint faith may illuminate the human experience of marriage. But any suggestion that there is a marriage which is differentiated by being 'Christian', as compared with any other sort, is theologically and pastorally at fault. As the Book of Common Prayer describes it, marriage is 'to be honourable among all men'. This implies that what God means marriage to be may be perceived in any marriage, whatever the particular beliefs of the partners.[6]

There is, therefore, every reason for Christian ministers and churches to remain open for people to explore the significance of marriage, of their relationship, and of the intention expressed through the rite. For the rite conveys its own message to people, not least that marriage is a public act of divinely created beings, which, even when most marred and apparently deficient, has something to do with God's intentions.

It is in this light that ministers need to consider second

marriages. Different churches have their own disciplines. But often the decision comes down to what the local minister is or is not willing to do. He or she will always find that the church tensions described above come down to personal strain on the minister. Two practical points may well be held in mind. First, in any marriage, the celebrants are the couple themselves. If, then, they determine to marry, then they marry. What is more, the church recognizes the marriage, even if it does not take place in church. Ministers, therefore, who are instinctively and initially reluctant at last to consider participating in such a wedding might examine themselves first before considering the couple. Second, as with all these occasional offices, the contemporary context in which the Christian churches offer such ministry is highly confused. The question of attitude to ministry thus also becomes acute. The argument in this book is that precisely because things are confused, the church should stay as strongly in the field as it can and not surrender any point of contact with people. If, then, ministers refuse opportunities for intimate involvement with people, the churches should not complain that their message about God, the meaning of life and personal relations is ignored.

The Approach

The minister may conduct many weddings each year, but every one is unique for the couple. A crucial notion, which all involved in the approach phase need to grasp, is that the couple are not the ministers of the rite only in an ideal sense. They actually are and have to be. They, therefore, have to be encouraged consistently to take their responsibility.

Couples approach the church in a variety of emotional states, which may be summarized as 'disarray'. The step of coming to book a wedding may be the first joint act that the couple perform where their behaviour and intentions become public to a person in authority whom they do not know. Hitherto they have been involved with friends, people at work, possibly the jeweller, and their families. To these they can relate without too much difficulty, because they have some idea of the assumptions that are being made about them. This is even true of any meeting with a doctor or lawyer. To book the wedding, however, puts their proposed relationship in a new light. Nervousness and anxiety may, therefore, seem disproportionate to the act. They are also approaching a church about which they will have some fantasies.[7] Today, for example, the chances are that the couple will be living together. A reason for marrying may be either the imminence of a child or the wish to start a family legitimately. Questions of sexual behaviour have probably been faced long ago. But fantasies remain strong about the church and its attitude to sexual morality. Clergy often report a general sense of nervous guilt on the couple's part, which makes it difficult for them to express what they wish to request or to engage in a serious conversation with a stranger, especially a vicar. The woman may be pregnant, and some primitive feelings of uncleanness or even wrong may be present. The man may have been able to appear proud of his virility with his colleagues, but this seems less wise a stance in front of a clergyman.

A further range of pressures derives from the family, which may contain members of different generations and a variety of assumptions about marriage. Marriage as an institution and people's expectation of it are different from what they have been in recent generations.[8] The idea of marriage remains constant, but the word shrouds the differences. What, for example, seems to the family another step in the generations, with the implication that the marriage will lead to children, may be to the couple a powerfully counter-cultural act. In coming to church they may be meeting expectations of doing what is proper. But by doing something which is also unusual, they may be creating widespread unease. An unsuspected contributor to this may be television. For this enables people to believe that they have lived aspects of life and had experiences before they themselves can have them. The actual experience then takes on an aura of *déjà vu*.[9] Put together these many factors contribute to a sense of incomprehensible conflict, which is often found around a wedding: parents and especially grandparents think of marriage as a new state, which cannot be experienced until it is reached; but the couple may reckon that they already know, through actual and believed experience, about this state, so that the wedding is a ratification of what already exists. And the whole mélange is compounded with the set of models that is already built into each partner, which derive from their close observation of their parents' marriages.

In the light of all this the sensitive minister may be wary during this approach phase of quickly inviting the couple to join groups or intimate discussions with other couples, whether contemporaries or older. That may well be appropriate later. At this stage the task is more limited: to begin enabling the couple to become publicly responsible for their present relationship and their forthcoming marriage. Exploring their anxieties, whether these take the form of hopes or fears constitutes the bulk of the exploration. But for them to move to that position, some technical points need efficient handling during this phase. The law on marriage is strict and the minister has a professional duty to be sure about it. In most instances there is no problem, but the signs which warn of potential alarms should be deliberately checked at this stage. Among the obvious signals are whether a person has been divorced, which matters both for the law (in order to avoid bigamy) and for some churches. Age is another question. Non-British nationality requires careful attention. There is also the time scale for reading the banns and, if necessary, procuring the licence.[10]

Other less obviously technical matters arise. They may appear trivial to the minister, but loom large to the couple. For example, arrangements for a reception often dictate other requirements. The minister has to be clear about dates and times. Confirmation in writing may seem burdensome, but is normal, and sensible, practice in business. The couple may also have questions about protocol with which the minister can help. But he needs to take care lest he begins, from the best of motives, to collude with their expectations and be made into an expert on things about which he can have no knowledge.

Some advocate leaving these matters until a marriage interview or preparation meeting. This seems unwise. Marriage preparation is concerned more with serious issues and should operate in an area of greater profundity than merely removing technical problems. If the minor anxieties of the couple (which may feel major to them) are not dealt with at this early opportunity, the assurance that could be theirs may be missing from later engagements with the church and its ministers. As they invite people to assume responsibility for their affairs as mature human beings, ministers are obliged to assist them in discovering what it is that they are managing.

Exploring the Meaning

In his work on marital counselling Dr Jack Dominian has outlined five dimensions for every marriage.[11] Not all will necessarily be handled competently, but account has to be taken of each. These are: social, intellectual, spiritual, sexual and emotional. Some sense of the new social unit being created and appreciation of the roles which depend on it is required, together with some compatibility between intellectual gifts and a shared sense of values. Sex is today considered a barometer for what is valued or lacking in a couple's life, and the mention of the emotional facet directs attention to the contemporary approach to marriage as an enriching human relationship. The minister could usefully take this framework for exploring the meaning of marriage in this occasional office. Each area is one in which each partner has to take individual responsibility and in which shared developments must occur. But these are not headings to be imposed as a check list. Once again, what the minister holds within herself to give shape to her work with the couple, is the key factor in exploring the meaning of marriage with those about to embark on it.

There is a contemporary vogue for training. Any problem, so it is believed, may be resolved, provided sufficient training is offered. But training is a dispiriting notion with which to confront those seeking to acknowledge publicly through marriage their relationship of mutual affection and love. It also implies that there is information or a technique which can be supplied by some who have it to those who lack. But such a feeling is the last that a couple facing this enterprise need engendered in them. Training for marriage, therefore, is not a useful model for the church's ministry at this juncture. But because the church is involved in weddings, it believes that it should offer some form of marriage preparation. This may be true, but it has to be noted that it is impossible adequately to handle in depth a lifetime's beliefs and observations, not to mention personal feelings and attitudes, during the pressured time that is available to couples between the moment that they approach the church for a service and the wedding itself. If the minister and the church are seriously to consider preparation for marriage, then this has to be part of a long-term programme of contributing to schools and other groups, not to mention its political involvement in national and local programmes.

That said, however, the couple coming for a wedding might reasonably expect their relationship and their expectations of it to stand some scrutiny from each other with the help of the minister. Marriage preparation is widely discussed at present. It ranges from extensive courses to a brief interview with the minister. What is done locally will depend upon a series of factors, such as the culture and its norms and the number of weddings in which the minister is occupied. In order, however, to explore their relationship and the significance of their intention to marry the couple need opportunities. One option might be a chance to talk separately with the minister. Ministers tend to affirm the couple as an already existent unit. But however intimate the couple may be, there remains for them a transition through public ritual to a new status. A range of responses have brought them to this point. If, however, they are to have a chance to act responsibly, a brief time for each to examine alone with the minister his or her personal expectations and motivations could be valuable and advisable. Very occasionally one partner may feel that the proposed marriage is a mistake. The pastor's role then would become helping each individual and the couple together to discover what this admission implies. Such work, whatever the outcome, demands time and organization. This is difficult, but the minister's attention will say more about the church's attitude to marriage than many a pronouncement or report.

Some churches have inaugurated courses and group work. But however sophisticated they are, it is not a replacement for a discussion between the church's minister and those who are to be the celebrants at the wedding. For the focus of this meeting is ministry: what rite they will solemnize; how this illuminates their relationship; and how this may provide a basis for continuing—hopefully lifelong—scrutiny and support. The relationship which the two have already created and from which the marriage is to grow, is not something which may casually be assumed to be material for group discussion. Marriage preparation groups are sometimes offered as if they were compulsory. The value of some such meeting is widely attested, and often couples come to appreciate diligent work with them along with other couples. But such learning depends upon the couple consenting to take part. Attendance at such meetings cannot be a precondition for eligibility to be married in church. Therefore any exploration of the meaning of the rite has to be mutually agreed between the minister and the couple.

There is no question about an interview with the couple. This concentrates upon the nature of their relationship and how they might try and express it, the wider significance of human love, and the resources available within them and to them to enable their marriage to grow. It is also an occasion for fostering by interpretation the notion of and need for communication between each of them. One area, however, which is often avoided by mutual consent, is that of conflict. Competent handling of conflict is a major factor in emotional maturing and is one for which couples in contemporary culture often seem unprepared. To discuss this question reminds the couple of the realities of the step that they are about to take. The minister will particularly assist by representing to them the public context within which they will be establishing their marriage. He may be able to hold on their behalf the idea of a transition that requires some management. This will also help him clarify a difference between his own public ministry and marital counselling. Those to be married come into contact with a wide range of experts, who all claim to know what should be done—parents, florists, caterers, doctors, car hire firms, and so on—and cannot proceed without them. But the church, which reminds the couple that they and no one else is responsible, is not another such expert. It may, by avoiding the trap of behaving as one, then provide a valuable holding environment within which the couple, both as an entity and as individuals, may find during a time of stress and disarray the momentary space to take up their public and private roles.[12]

During the 1950s churches began to provide informative

courses for those about to be married. They comprised
sessions for a group of couples, at which practical advice
would be offered. People like estate agents, bank mana-
gers, doctors and priests would take part. Some, however,
increasingly feel that such courses are neither desirable
nor necessary. If marriage is regarded as a relationship
which is expected to develop, then opportunities are
needed to examine the nature of such a relationship and its
potential. The Roman Catholic Marriage Advisory Council,
for example, offers such a programme. If no such course
is available, local bodies, such as Relate, are usually willing
to assist ministers in creating one. Much, however, seems
to depend upon the sophistication of those involved. In
some parishes ministers point out that social customs do
not include discussion, least of all on private life. They
also note that the provision of basic information in a
course is still valuable and may constitute an entry to
larger issues, not least where the roles of the partners
are highly stereotyped. For example, a woman who has
never had to manage a house-keeping budget, but is
expected at marriage to be able to do so, may be relieved to
find others in the same predicament. And on that base
may be erected a structure for examining the expectations
that the partners have of each other and the reasons for
them.

In each of these areas judgement has to be made in the
light of the minister's perception of how the task of
exploring meaning may best be performed. The aim,
however, in each case remains consistently simple: to
enable the couple, separately and together, to compre-
hend what they already know of themselves and of each
other, so that they may confidently undertake the rite of
marrying each other.

The Rite

The key to interpreting a wedding is to recognize that the
couple are the officiants and that the minister facilitates
their ministry and blesses it. Any theology of marriage
which is expressed liturgically, therefore, will primarily
be one which expounds the human institution of marriage and illuminates its divine facets by means of the
Christian gospel. In the Anglican tradition this accounts

for the fact that the marriage rite has, as Geoffrey Cuming points out, 'been more gently revised than any other'.[13] Since this is a human rite, it will not change very much in the light of liturgical discoveries, but will mildly develop as that which people need to express alters. A small example may be seen in the way in which the custom of the man giving the woman a ring has been changed to that of giving and receiving a ring on the part of each, which has now been liturgically legitimized.

Since the couple are the ministers, they have responsibility for the ritual and its performance. This is sometimes forgotten by clergy, not least in their wish to avoid disputes and, on occasion, to pacify church officers, vergers and, in particular, organists. Michael Perham reminds the minister that he is not the arbiter of taste, but that 'the chief pastoral need is to help them to relax and to feel assured that the service is in safe hands'.[14] This is true, but the safe hands are, so far as possible, first those of the couple. It follows that, although sometimes families may be invited to participate, the working relationship is between the couple and the church through the minister. The service, as part of the process, can be discussed during the final stages of exploring the meaning of marriage, and the liturgy may be used as a check against which the couple's reflections and aspirations can be tested. If it appears to express something that they do not wish to acknowledge for themselves, then there is a matter requiring study, since this probably indicates an unresolved issue between or around the couple. It does not, however, in the outcome necessarily follow that the liturgy remains unaltered. There is a wide variety of options available in modern service books.

Details of how to manage a wedding are available in various manuals. One major stance, however, is worth the minister's attention. Marriage as an instance of mutual self-giving and personal relationship is now expressed in the modern liturgies. Its public significance, however, is less apparent. In the rite the minister's presence is a reminder of God's intention for the couple and for his whole creation. In a sense, therefore, he stands especially for the social implications of the marriage at a point where the personal investment is felt most keenly. An incumbent in the Church of England, as registrar, has to occupy this place legally by having to ensure that the correct procedures are followed. But his task is also to enlarge the significance of that love which is exemplified in the couple, however adequately or inadequately. *Ubi caritas et amor, Deus ibi est.* God's love is wider than the love expressed in this one instance, yet for a moment this one instance also encapsulates that wideness and divine generosity. If this aspect is missing from the wedding, the rite is deficient. The couple cannot be expected to hold such a perspective unaided. In devising the ritual with the couple, he will introduce ideas from this angle, which the couple may then be able to pursue. The obvious examples are hymns, scripture readings and, if there are any, other readings.

The issue increasingly arises of an appropriate marriage rite when a divorced person is involved. Those churches which perform such marriages have their own proposals. For those which at present do not, there is a service of blessing. This is a theological nonsense, but it may for the time being be pastorally necessary and effective. Three points may be noted. First, whatever the minister's views on marriage and divorce, he or she represents the churches' confusion. The minister, therefore, has to be sensitive lest his own and the church's muddle is projected into vulnerable people. Secondly, there is a more technical matter. With the ease of world-wide travel and different approaches to divorce in various countries, it is becoming increasingly complicated to disentangle the legal questions as to who is eligible to be married under British law. Any minister, therefore, intending to conduct a wedding, as opposed to a blessing, for a divorced person should be wary and check the details with the Registrar. And thirdly, whatever the rights or wrongs, there seems nothing in principle different in the process of ministering with a couple, one or both of whom has been divorced, than with those approaching matrimony for the first time.

Feed-back

Of the occasional offices a wedding is the one where those concerned are most likely to move away. Problems of housing and employment often make this inevitable. A consequence is that the couple have to develop their new relationship in some isolation from familiar surroundings and friends. This may be a contributory factor to the intensely personal understanding of marriage that prevails and which make marriages potentially fragile as institutions.

To leave the matter there, however, would be to fall into the trap of thinking that the one-to-one connection is the only important aspect of a brief encounter. How the minister acts in these offices is more widely known than he may suspect and it influences other facets of his ministry. He may receive direct feed-back from the friends and relations of the couple. More importantly, because he is known to be concerned with marrying, he may also be expected from time to time to comment on marriage and counsel married people. This is not a book on such counselling, and the point may merely be noted. If, however, adequate attention is given by the minister to his public role in the performance of the rite, then the future of marriages as human institutions will also be affected. Too easily the counselling response attracts ministers. Jack Dominian notes the danger of this seduction, when he calls his chapter on marriage preparation 'Preventing Breakdown'.[15] The concern which pastors demonstrate for acquiring skills in counselling marital breakdown may itself be evidence for a loss of confidence in the more mundane role of minister, as this has been described. But the question needs to be asked as to the extent to which abdication from their role in the occasional office may indicate that ministers are inadvertently contributing to marital breakdown. There is not much point in learning how to quench fires that one is lighting oneself.

Most weddings are celebrations. Even if they are not, the powerful investment in the couple may allow all concerned, including the minister, to overlook issues that are aroused. High on the list are questions of authority and guilt. Marriage in western society brings together in a unique way both private and social issues. It is, therefore, difficult for people to sort these out in themselves and in their relationships. The emphasis in this discussion on pastoral work has been on affirming the couple's authority, their individual responsibility for their decision to marry, and their joint responsibility as ministers of the sacrament. Problems of authority and its exercise are endemic in contemporary society. If, however, people are believed to be created in the image of God, as the Judaeo-Christian tradition consistently avows, then the nature of this assigned authority is a vital concern. This is especially so if the concept of 'the image of God' is linked to the primal pair of male and female. To be made in this image is to be given authority to be human. Yet that authority is constantly diminished or perverted. This comprises the essence of the doctrine of sin. As people approach marriage, a pervading sense is one of disarray, anxiety, sometimes unworthiness and even guilt. It may be argued that the church itself induces that guilt, but, whatever the church's contribution, it seems more likely that some such guilt is felt as human beings approach the creation of a new human institution for which they have to take public responsibility. In other words, weddings raise the issue of debased and refused authority in human beings, and one of the ministries sought from the church is forgiveness for failure and absolution. This is no simple matter of confession and ritual absolution. But we may understand such forgiveness as the reaffirmation on God's part that the authority which he assigns to all his creatures really is theirs. They are given it and invited confidently to act upon it.

It may be, therefore, that the church, when it encounters individuals and couples for a wedding, may be ministering to more profound matters, which belong to all men and women. The feed-back from this occasional office consequently may be more than a response from the couple or their relations and friends. It may become a key constituent for the grasp of ministry as a whole, with which the church and its ministers operate in a locality. If so, weddings become far more than a chore. They are instances for the acting out of God's trust in his creatures and the discovery of that authority which he has assigned to his creatures, both individually and socially. Properly perceived, therefore, weddings offer opportunities for all involved to explore what it means to be human in the light of God's revelation. They are of the essence of Christian ministry.

Notes

1. The Church of England produced two major reports (see chapter 4 above). Note also Pope John Paul II, *Familiaris Consortio* (London, Catholic Truth Society, 1981). On the changes in expectations see S. Dowell, *They Two shall be One: Monogamy in History and Religion* (London, Collins, 1990).
2. W. K. Lowther Clarke, 'Solemnisation of Matrimony', in W. K. Lowther Clarke ed., *Liturgy and Worship* (London, SPCK, 1932), pp. 458ff.
3. M. Green, *Marriage* (London, Fontana, 1984); J. Dominian, *Passionate and Compassionate Love* (London, Darton, Longman and Todd, 1991).
4. On the impact of the pair in any setting see W. R. Bion, *Experiences in Groups* (London, Tavistock, 1969), pp. 111ff.
5. S. Platten, 'The Church's response to current divorce trends', *Crucible* (1984), pp. 82ff.
6. *Marriage, Divorce and the Church*, p. 14.
7. The word 'fantasy' is used in a general sense to refer to wish, always in the end informed by the unconscious, which is distorted by defensive processes.
8. G. Gorer, *Sex and Marriage in England Today* (London, Nelson, 1971). *Marriage and the Church's Task*, pp. 17ff.
9. C. Morris, *God-in-a-Box* (London, Hodder, 1984), pp. 25ff. For a more developed discussion see W. Carr, *Ministry and the Media* (London, SPCK, 1990).
10. P. Chambers, *Made in Heaven?* (London, SPCK, 1988). Technical information can always be obtained from the local registrar.
11. J. Dominian, *Make or Break* (London, SPCK, 1984), ch. 8.
12. The notion of a holding environment derives from the care-taking function of parents.
13. G. J. Cuming, *A History of Anglican Liturgy*, 2nd edition (London, Macmillan, 1982), p. 220.
14. Perham, *Liturgy*, p. 97.
15. Dominian, *Make or Break*, ch. 19.

EIGHT

Funerals

━━━━

When baptizing, the minister has to face a series of theological problems about the nature of the gospel and its relation to everyday human experience. Confronted by those who wish to marry, his difficulty may be seen in terms of authority: if they are the officiants, what exactly is his role? Funerals, at least in the urban setting, present him with a sense that his theology and his authority are both swamped by the power of the emotion of grief and its social accompaniments.

There is a host of books about death, grief and mourning. Training officers report increased eagerness on the part of clergy to attend courses on bereavement counselling. It is difficult to participate in any gathering of clergy at which stories of funerals and half-serious jokes about undertakers (not to mention funeral fees) are not told. But if churches exist through interaction with their environment, we should not be surprised to find such matters becoming prominent. It is a modern commonplace (although not an accurate one) that, whereas the Victorians were preoccupied with death, twentieth-century man has become obsessed with sex. But such is the rate of change in society that even attitudes towards death and bereavement seem to alter rapidly. Since ministry is always exercised in a social context, the church's ministry through funerals will itself be subject to similar change.

The 1960s and 1970s were a period of optimism in many ways. Sexuality may have become a more prominent issue. Sanction was certainly given for a variety of behaviours which were characterized as 'the permissive society'. But in that setting death and its associated rituals became an embarrassment for many. It was not a taboo subject, but nor was it one which attracted interest. At one level customs disappeared—the wearing of black as a matter of respect, armbands, and raising the hat as a hearse passed. On a different plane the imminence of death as a result of nuclear war was ignored, except by campaigners, whose number decreased. In that environment some professional people, however—psychoanalysts, psychologists, doctors and journalists—were constrained to stress the importance of being able to face death, the place of ritual, and the care needed by the bereaved.[1] Twenty years later those books came into their own. Medical developments have made people unsure of what constitutes death and even when it occurs. Commonsense ideas about death have been displaced by a sense that personal mortality is in the hands of technicians. Megadeaths, a new coinage, are now a factor in people's thinking, which leads to a corresponding fatalism. In every way death is a prominent issue in contemporary society. As a result, the particular deaths which occur and which generate the grief with which the minister is confronted, may carry other anxieties and anguishes.

Life's final transition is into the unknown. All other transitions reflect this ultimate separation. Death provides the basic model. But equally these other, intermediate separations inform the way that that model is construed. So, for example, people are aware that the world could be destroyed. Change in society seems to devalue what has been achieved in the past. The uncertainty of death itself is compounded by these additional factors, which contribute to a heightened level of anxiety.[2] Interest in spiritualism and the respectability now accorded to studies of existence after death do little to alter the basic issue for the minister.[3] This is that people look to a symbolic figure to have assurance and claim knowledge, which in the nature of the case no human being can possess.

In conducting funerals the minister is caught up in a greater range of issues than might immediately be apparent. Some of these are within him, as a human being who has to face his own death. But he will probably have only the most fleeting and almost professionally ritualistic contact with the bereaved, and probably none at all with the dying. When allowed to minister to a dying person, pastors today count it a rare privilege. It is, therefore, with the inevitably brief encounter of the funeral service that we are concerned. The grief of the family is the point of contact.

This chapter is not intended to supplement the already large literature on bereavement counselling and the pastoral care of the dying and the bereaved. This is discussed only as it affects the occasional office of the funeral. Although there are signs of an increasing demand for non-religious funerals, most are still conducted by a minister of religion. It is disputed whether this is because of the lack of easily available alternatives or because there is even in the most apparently irreligious a sense that there is here a mystery that needs appropriate handling. Sometimes pastors are invited to take the funeral of a person of another faith. They are certainly accustomed to ministering to those of no obvious belief. The minister seems to represent something significant, albeit something of which most remain at a conscious level ignorant. Stories abound which demonstrate that his is a complex role, which is largely delineated by others. He is, for example, believed to be able to manage this final boundary to life. This may be a residual belief from the days when he would have been called to assist the dying to depart from this world. Clergy are still surprised to find that elderly people may regard a house communion as an implied viaticum and accordingly refuse the offer. But the minister is seen as more than a manager of such things. He is also looked to as a person of professed faith, who is believed to be able to face the spectre of death and, as it were, to defeat it. He is expected to be competent, even though he knows in himself that he is as human as anyone else. His believed strength in the face of death and his ability to be able to handle it produce a curious amalgam in people's minds, whereby he may almost become the purveyor of death, the death-man. As such he is both needed and shunned. These, and similar fantasies, make the minister a potent symbol in the context of death. By contrast, his own struggle with his faith and his humanity consistently remind him of his weakness and vulnerability. The pressure upon him, therefore, is to respond by acting a part, so that he may meet the expectations of his audience and not be hurt himself. There is probably no future in such a stance for any human being, and certainly for Christian ministry it has no profit.

The minister, when summoned for a funeral, joins a

process at a specific point. Studies of bereavement have shown how lengthy the total process is, even though in our society ritualized mourning is brief. The clergyman may be assigned about half an hour for the ritual and possibly a little more for an associated visit. But mourning lasts between two and five years, and the first two weeks, during which the minister's involvement occurs, is the time of greatest shock, denial and numbness.[4] In order to find his bearings in this context, the minister may use a generalized theory of the bereavement process. One danger, however, is that he may inadvertently become glib about death. Being able, as he believes, to locate a bereaved person within a theoretical construction, may suggest that he has accurately diagnosed their condition. The minister may then isolate himself by applying the appropriate 'treatment'. This is a caricature of ministry, but one which is occasionally met. It is almost as if the old defensive professionalism of the priest, who reads a standard service, has given place to a new form of so-called 'caring professionalism', by which the 'patient' is identified, diagnosed and treated. Understanding of the process, which may help provide the minister with an internal frame of reference, is useful only as a means of assisting him locate himself in relation to each particular individual and unique bereavement.

Although within the long and varied process of bereavement the funeral occupies only a little time, its significance is disproportionate to its length. The funeral in practice takes place early in the period of mourning. It, therefore, crystallizes the immediate realities, such as the fact that someone actually has died and that the living have to do something about it. At the same time, in the confused dislocations of death, it provides a reference point to which people can and do refer, as they work out their sense of bereavement. It becomes part of the folk-lore of the family, or, to use another metaphor, one of the sets of spectacles through which the dead person is remembered. What shape, therefore, those spectacles take is important for the lives of those reintegrating themselves into everyday life.[5]

This simple observation reinforces an obvious but important point about this rite: the funeral is for the bereaved and not for the corpse. The minister is not dismissing a soul from this world, nor is she merely disposing of mortal remains. She is not dealing with 'death' as some abstract phenomenon. She is in touch with a human experience of profound significance, which all have to undergo—the experience of loss and bereavement. The funeral, therefore, is for those who are left. Their emotions are being handled, and that perspective will naturally colour what is done in each instance.

The Approach

The funeral is quite unlike the other two offices in the approach phase. There are no parents seeking something for their child, or a couple looking for an opportunity for themselves. The usual approach to a minister comes as the result of something that has already occurred and is complete in itself: the person has died; the family are coping; the undertaker has the details in hand; and then the minister is contacted, usually by the undertaker. This contact with the bereaved is mediated. That fact may affect the relationship that may be established between the minister and the bereaved. For he may appear to be an imposed necessity and may feel himself to be such. He is there because a funeral has to be performed. Often he is not known or in any personal sense wanted.

This all creates obvious tensions. Relationships take time and there is usually no time, especially in a busy parish. The bereaved themselves are in a distressed state and probably do not feel like making a new relationship with a stranger, albeit a needed one. And inevitably expectations of the encounter will be coloured by half-remembered experiences from previous times of grief and from impressions given by the undertaker. For most people the experience of bereavement is chaotic. One effect of people's being generally unfamiliar with death and how to deal with it, even at a formal level, is that they tend to surrender their responsibilities to others, who take them over effectively, swiftly and competently. But in so doing they deprive people of their own authority and responsibility as relatives of one who has died. At the same time such efficiency may enable the bereaved to feel fine, since any other burdens in addition to grief seem unnecessarily harsh. But in the long run this relief can have a deleterious effect, as people develop an irrational sense of guilt that they should have done more, been more deeply involved, or looked after the deceased better. The minister, as a so-called 'expert', may have a constructive role in this phase. She is brought in because she knows about funerals. But many of the arrangements for that funeral will not be in her hands. She may take this as a personal slight and fight for a position of more acknowledged competence among the group of those who are handling the bereavement. On the other hand, she may acknowledge her freedom to represent ultimate human issues of responsibility in a chaotic context of experience, and thus use the occasion for effective (which is not the same as efficient) ministry.

The task of this approach phase within the sequence of the funeral arrangements may be described as that of enabling the bereaved to become conscious of their grief process in which they are caught up. This is their responsibility as human beings and in their roles as relatives or friends of the deceased. To facilitate this, however, there are a number of points to which the minister may attend.

Early in the bereavement those responsible for making the funeral arrangements have much to consider. Most funeral directors are careful in guiding them through the legal and other requirements that follow a death. There are many of these, and people often comment on the sense of rush that results. The days seem like a race to get things done in time for the funeral; the nights are long and, especially for a widow or widower, lonely. The British are said to be poor at facing the need to grieve and express feelings. In this maelstrom of activity the bereaved need space in which to grieve and on occasions permission to do so. The prevailing culture tends to diminish death. The euphemisms and the reassurances that it is somehow unreal are familiar. One consequence is that grieving may be omitted at the early stage of loss. The minister, as the 'death person', is often the one who can give permission to grieve. The funeral, for which he is needed, is an occasion for public grieving, whatever else it may be. It is the final leave-taking from all that was tangible of a human being, whose life affected others. To facilitate this process the minister needs to listen when he meets the relatives of the deceased, and especially members of the wider family. If he can begin to discern tensions and conflicts, as well as expressions of hope and unsuspected affection, he may be able to construct in his own mind a rough grid of relationships and so place the deceased within it. This will assist him to imbue the formality of grieving in the course of the funeral with necessary reality.

During this phase the minister is also expected to manage certain things. The pressure upon him is to collude with disowning behaviour on the part of the bereaved, which shows itself in a desire to leave the details of the funeral to the minister. However understandable such attitudes may seem in the emotion of the moment, and however much the caring dimension of the minister may instinctively respond to it, this has to be resisted. Ritual, especially that surrounding death, is not merely a containing framework for human grief, to which it is applied with more or less skill by the minister. It is created by those concerned —the bereaved and the more detached symbolic figure of the minister—as a means of enabling a major transition to be accomplished. Bereaved people at an early stage experience shock and denial. Their lives feel deformed and shapeless. In that setting the funeral liturgy may provide a framework which, however little it is consciously appreciated, may nevertheless assure people that there is some shape to human existence which can be recovered. But if the ritual is to perform this function, then the bereaved have also to begin to make it their own.

A small illustration is that of the role of chief mourner, who often comes into his own at the reception after the funeral. The minister is often invited to this, but when there is ignored. It is as if the host or hostess, as chief mourner, somehow takes over from the minister the role of providing shape to life by emphasizing the familiar and customary. If, then, the bereaved are to make the earlier ritual of the funeral their own, too, they not only need information about the options available but also to sense the partnership with the minister, so that they can authorize him to act on their behalf as well as for the larger unknowns of society, humanity and God. His theological and spiritual resource for sustaining such a role may thus be made available to the bereaved.

Exploring the Meaning

Since the encounter with people during this occasional office is so brief, it is not possible (except for the sake of discussion) to separate this second phase from the approach. The minister may on rare occasions have already established a relationship which allows the meaning of bereavement and death to be explored before, during and after the funeral. But for most this is a luxury. In today's very brief encounter the chances are that only one pre-funeral visit may be possible. Since people are not likely to be able to take in very much at such a time, it follows that one of the chief tasks in this phase is to allow them to express as much as they wish or are able. In order to give permission to grieve, the minister holds certain realities on behalf of the bereaved. This is more difficult than it sounds, since there often appears to be an expectation that he will confirm their fantasies. As a human being he, too, will be to some degree uncertain about questions of death and its meaning. And even if he holds that his gospel provides him with certainties, he will not be able, for reasons which will become apparent, to present an apologia for them in the hope of sharing them at this stage with bereaved people.

The most difficult reality to face is that the dead person has died. For that reason the minister has to be unafraid of employing words like 'dead' or 'died'. This is particularly important for the funeral of a Christian believer. Much contemporary Christianity seems to regard death as a temporary break in life, and in so doing conforms to popular superstition rather than to the gospel. The minister has in the doctrine of the resurrection of the body an acknowledgement of death's reality. Tom Baker has expressed this succinctly:

> The doctrine of the resurrection of the body (of the whole person, if you like) authenticates our sense of poignant loss, because it is concerned precisely with the transformation of what has been lost. Nostalgia is often trivial and self-indulgent. But it is a very human emotion, and points to something real, of which we need not feel ashamed.[6]

The minister may have his own understanding of an

approach to life and death, crucifixion and resurrection. But for the ministry which he is offering to the bereaved, this is a resource for assisting them to face the reality of death and not a means of colluding in avoiding it.

A second facet of the exploration is enabling people to realize that the process on which they have embarked is a long one. Immediate understanding, therefore, is not merely unlikely: it is impossible. Permission to grieve thus becomes something more than allowing people to cry. It is also encouraging them to recognize that, as a result of the deceased having died, there is a permanent, long-term felt loss, which the bereaved may try to fill in a number of ways. These may be in trying to deal with the residue of the relationship through other (usually unsuitable) people or in seeing visions. The content of this period of mourning is often very general. Bereaved people are not usually able to focus on specifics. But this is itself one means of allowing themselves space in the busyness of preparation for the funeral, so that through reflection they may provide for themselves points to which to refer back as they journey through the bereavement process.

One pressure on ministers at this point is to make statements that they cannot justify or promises that they cannot keep. Asked 'Will I see my loved one again, when I die?', he is inclined to soothe by answering affirmatively. But pastoral sensitivity and theological perception both demand a gentle 'No'. Some parts of the deceased person have gone for ever: the body is decaying, and as a result the relationship of embodied people is ended.[7] Belief in the resurrection of the body is no reason to deny, or imply that it is desirable to deny, the actual sense of ending, loss and permanence of death. The minister may also wish to assure the bereaved of divine care by promising what he cannot fulfil. One customary guarantee is that he will make a post-funeral visit. Sometimes such a call can be valuable, and this is discussed later. But for most clergy these visits are a sheer impossibility. To promise one, therefore, or even appear to, is probably the minister's self-protection. Rather than an instance of genuine pastoral activity, such a suggestion merely creates further unreality in the situation.

The key to the exploration phase of a funeral is the way

in which the minister manages himself in role. The emotional impact of the encounter is greater than in the case of the other offices. Because of the way that our society handles death, the temptation before the minister is to defend against any intrusion into his own self by adopting an apparently professional role. In this ministry, however, the pastor brings his own human and spiritual vulnerability to bear with people at their most fragile. The separation of death may be compared with a stripping off of part of oneself or even of separation from the self. In such a ministry, the minister is exposed to his own humanity. 'Every man's *death* diminishes *me*', and the minister who is regularly involved with death is bound to experience that diminishing.[8] To compensate he may seek counselling skills, although they are not really required. Alternatively he may look to invulnerable (as he believes) theological positions, which are immune from scrutiny or scepticism. The outcome, however, is a brittle person, whose reliability may feel suspect to those who seek some ministry.

One area in which such disturbance sometimes shows itself is in believed competition with funeral directors. Relationships between undertakers and ministers are inevitably close, if not intimate. Pastors may be so confined in their own self-perception that they may overlook the obvious fact that funeral directors are usually the first ministers in any bereavement, just as the police may take this role at a sudden or accidental death. To ignore or discount such ministries because they appear theologically unauthenticated limits the pastor's own ministering. Since, however, it is difficult to express to the bereaved, or with them, the strong feelings which a death generates in the pastor, there is a risk that these may be directed at the undertaker or back at oneself. In the former case, this can produce futile contretemps, which may make ministers feel better but which will not further overall ministry in an area. In the latter instance, this introverted anger may produce apathy, which then diverts energy from a vital piece of public ministry. In either case, a minister in the exploration phase of the encounter over a funeral might usefully ask himself what he is doing with his own powerful, human emotions.

The approach phase is essentially one of collaboration with the bereaved and with others, such as the undertaker. The minister may experience ambivalent feelings directed at him. On the one hand he may be treated almost as the only one who understands at any depth and can deal effectively with the death. If he colludes with that, he may not only diminish the bereaved people's responsibility and so not help them. He may also cease to work with others and find himself antipathetic to them. On the other hand, he may feel brought in as a necessary, but unfortunate factor, in the production of a funeral, which is mostly out of his hands and control. Some resentment at such an attitude is not unnatural, but it may become compounded by a sense of insult to his gospel of resurrection. To survive this felt onslaught, he may try and escape the human emotions which are his and so avoid encountering those of others. Either way, the minister may feel especially ineffective at this point in the bereavement process. If, however, he can grasp that such feelings are part of the complex and chaotic experience of bereavement, he may be able to discover through them what is happening. For he will be able to give direct attention to the practical question, which is a sure guide in all Christian ministry: 'What is happening to me, and why?' Self-interpretation in role is the clue to ministry in exploring the meaning of death and bereavement.[9]

The Rite

In thinking of funerals it is especially useful to distinguish between 'rite' and 'ritual'. The ritual is the funeral itself, with all its accompaniments—undertakers, flowers, minister, service in church or chapel, and wake or funeral tea. The rite, however, is a wider concept, covering the extended process of transition from the initial separation to reincorporation into society. The ritual plays a fundamental part in the rite. Because contemporary western society remains unsure about how to think of death and how people should behave in the face of it, a range of rituals has been created. Two, for example, concern the disposal of the corpse (burial or cremation) and the place where the ritual is held (church, crematorium or home). Although each of these options seems simple, they shroud a range of unexplored questions. Burial or cremation, for example, both dispose of the corpse but each conveys diverse images of value and employ different archetypes.

A funeral is a social occasion. Local customs vary, but associations extend beyond the family. Colleagues from work, miscellaneous social contacts, other friends and acquaintances, people from the street, are all likely to attend a funeral. Announcements of death still fill the personal columns in local newspapers. The funeral, which hitherto the minister might have thought about in terms of the family and the deceased, affects more people. As the family consider the service with the minister, this perspective may be lost. The pastor, therefore, may have deliberately to introduce it or at least hold on to it. For example, there is little point in an intimate family group wishing to sing a favourite, but obscure, hymn which the dead person enjoyed, when the minister knows that few, if any, of those attending from other backgrounds will know or understand it. There are other ways of incorporating such requests, as, for example, in a reading or as part of any music played. The family and more casual acquaintances will thus both be able to participate.

This minor example indicates the role of the minister in the funeral service. He directs it. There may be close collaboration in the design of the ritual, but its performance lies in the minister's hands. For the bereaved there are many discomforting aspects to a funeral, which range from feelings aroused by the final acknowledgement that the body has gone to anxieties about proper behaviour in public. Through the ritual the minister is asked to articulate on behalf of people what they cannot at this moment manage for themselves. The funeral, therefore, is a singular instance of managed worship.

Reflections on worship as an instance of managed regression illuminate the minister's task. The term 'regression' sounds pejorative but it well describes the process of such worship.[10] Human development is a progression from childhood and dependence upon parents to adult acknowledgement of interdependence between responsible people. Mature adults live in an oscillation between these two states of dependence and autonomy. Regression to dependence, therefore, is not a reversion to infantile behaviour, but an aspect of adult life, which requires affirmation and recognition. Worship and ritual provide specific occasions of and opportunity for controlled regression. Through ritual people may experience the surrender of sophisticated interpretation, or the facade that they are capable of this, and allow thoughts and feelings to range in a managed context of images and ideas. Considered in this light, a funeral service is not an event but a means by which a process may be undergone. In order to facilitate this regression and the move back towards recovery of responsibility and autonomy, a secure environment is created. Liturgy performs this function, both through the way in which it is conducted and with its unfamiliar richness of ideas and images. Impressions and conveyed ideas, especially at a funeral, are more important than precise words and intended meanings.

Bereaved people are disoriented. The minister is invited to stand for them on a boundary where they feel at present unable to stand and to manage a process on their behalf. Although such feelings are acute in the immediate family, the congregation will also include people at different stages of grief and with various degrees of involvement with the deceased. The minister cannot prescribe what should be experienced, but she creates a context in which people may integrate themselves in any needful fashion. To achieve this the minister presents the reality of death as a fact of human existence. She cannot employ distracting euphemisms. Pastors also articulate feelings on behalf of the bereaved, and among these will certainly be a sense of uncertainty, confusion and disarray. At the same time her job is to do this without letting it degenerate merely into an emotional outburst on their behalf. The awe of present reality does not obliterate the future, when for the bereaved life continues. The pastor's ability to do this depends upon the way the approach phase has been handled. But people, especially under stress, also surrender to her an alarming amount of power, which she has to hold with astuteness. As a Christian she may be tempted to respond with almost glib talk of life after death, rather than a profound exploration of the gospel emphasis that life is in the midst of death. The minister has, therefore, to be particularly sensitive in this ministry to the feelings of others and at the same time bold in taking risks of judgement. She has to prove reliable and dependable, but only in such a way that people may, through the ritual, begin to resume their own responsibilities.

How this is achieved in each instance will depend upon the people with whom the pastor is dealing and local conditions. One or two general points, however, may be listed. Inevitably a funeral will be affected by local customs. In preparing the service, therefore, the minister may have to negotiate them into the liturgy. It is, however, crucial that people, if they are to be able to use the process as an occasion for handling grief and preparing for the future, participate. Under the immediate stress of grief they sometimes ask the minister merely to do what is proper and to keep it short and simple. There is much to be said for both brevity and simplicity, not least in liturgy. But behind the request may lie an attempt to escape grieving, to which the pastor will give attention. Even within the limitations of an urban cremation service the minister has time available, the use of which can be planned. The congregation should participate in the service itself. To say together the Lord's Prayer or a short psalm may be the minimum. But people should not at this juncture be required to attempt even familiar words from memory, and for many there will probably be no such familiar texts. Few, if any, today know the Lord's Prayer by heart and none will probably be able to manage it in an agreed version. A text, therefore, is essential, and the congregation may need directing to it. Such guidance should also extend to posture. If the service is to be an occasion of such managed regression as has been described, it should not feel disrupted by too much movement. Clear directions on standing and sitting (kneeling is not often advisable) will assist people to experience the dislocation of parting without being diverted towards additional anxieties about how they should be behaving. The minister is managing the process, but not the people, in so acting.

Society's disarray with death emerges in the debate about the place where a funeral should be held. Some evidence is beginning to appear that people are increasingly dissatisfied with a service at a crematorium, but are unclear about what they wish to replace it. It may be, especially with the amount of travelling involved, that funerals should be encouraged in the deceased's locality— that is, the local church—and followed by committal at the crematorium or graveyard. It has been proposed by some that cremation should precede the funeral, but there seems little enthusiasm for this and the image of a funeral service around an urn, rather than the corpse, seems strange. It is, however, important that, whatever arrangements are made, the bereaved family should, as a general rule, watch the disposal of the body through burial or its reception to the crematorium. Any ritual which does not include this formal separation from mortal remains, is deficient.

For all mourners the service should allow three expressions of feeling and time for reflection on them. First there is the sense of thanksgiving. This must vary according to the circumstances of death, but there are few human beings who cannot be recalled without some thankfulness. In the resolution phase of bereavement people need to come to terms with their anger and resentments and with the fact that business with the deceased remains unsatisfactorily incomplete. Expression of thanksgiving is not the same as idealizing the deceased. His or her limitations and faults can be named, but they can be incorporated into critical thanksgiving. Secondly, time is needed to recall what the dead person was to those who are bereaved. This implies sorrow and joy, as well as a sense of fulfilment and loss. Such emotions can be expressed, if space is deliberately made for them in the funeral service. For this offers momentarily secure room for the legitimate examination of such feelings. Thirdly, there is the fact that everyone has to confront his or her own death. This particular dying, therefore, is to be set in the context of all human mortality. Which of the available liturgies best furthers these tasks is not a matter for theoretical dispute. The choice is one of pastoral judgement. It may be, as some report, that different liturgies are suitable for different occasions, and that their variety is a positive asset.

One specific question which concerns some ministers is whether (and if so, how) they are to preach at a funeral service. Each minister is responsible for the way in which he believes that the proclamation of the gospel is best served, and will make his own decision. Four general observations, however, may be offered.

First, how the gospel is verbalized and conceptualized is a matter of dispute, but Christians agree that it does not consist of words alone. At the centre of the Christian message is the Word, which could only be encountered when it became enfleshed. Words are acknowledged, but not overvalued. The primary proclamation of the gospel in a funeral, whatever the minister may or may not articulate, will be the confidence that he embodies in the face of death. Because of the emotional dislocation experienced by the bereaved, they can rarely hear what is actually said. Odd remarks may stick, but people remember demeanour and attitude more than content. The reason for this is that at the time of the funeral bereaved people are struggling to create a structure for their survival. For that they will use whatever reinforces resources that are already within them. To ask them at this moment to adopt an unfamiliar structure is to invite its rejection. If, then, the minister feels in himself the general human sense of mortality, which any death generates, and embodies in himself the hope that his gospel holds out within that mortality, then he will chiefly convey this through the way he manages the process and the manner in which he conducts the ritual.

Secondly, the gospel itself is more vulnerable in the area of death than its ministers sometimes recognize. The Christian message has a tendency to gloss over death in its haste to reach the so-called joys of the resurrection. Any minister needs to guard against this theological weakness in his message. Early use, for example, of the traditional opening sentence of the liturgy—'I am the resurrection and the life' (John 11.25f)—raises the question. On the one hand its familiarity may be part of the reassurance of the funeral for the bereaved. On the other hand, its early affirmation of resurrection and life may detract from the opportunities to face the actual death of the deceased. A preferable logical progression might be: the reality of death; the everlasting love of God; God's grace made known in Christ; and the Christian hope for all mankind.[11] In the face of uncertainty about death, the liturgy requires some clear statement that death is not a failure, but a natural outcome to every human life, none of which can lie beyond God's mercy.

A further dangerous area theologically forms the third point. It is easily said, but is certainly not believable at the time of bereavement, that Jesus has undergone the same trauma as the bereaved. There is no evidence, other than as may be hinted by the extended story of Lazarus (John 11), that Jesus might have been bereaved. And bereavement is the focal issue in a funeral, rather than death. If ministers, in their preoccupation to present a relevant Christ, attempt it in this way, they will succeed in the very fault which they are trying to avoid. For they will depersonalize the ritual and make it less immediate for the bereaved, by appearing to suggest that their specific grief is merely an instance of some supposed greater grief, which was experienced on their behalf by Jesus Christ.

Finally, and most obviously, since it is not likely that those attending a funeral will be able to take in very much, the address, if there is to be one, has to be felt to be an intrinsic component of the liturgy and not an imposed extra. It will, therefore, be brief, carefully prepared, specific in its mention of the deceased and his or her family, and consciously structured into the particular funeral that is being conducted. If it is impossible to give such an address, as is often the case with duty funerals in a city crematorium, then it may be wiser to omit it and take greater care with the content of the service, the way people are guided through the ritual, and the prayers which are offered.

Feed-back

Since the process of grieving is lengthy, some sort of post-funeral contact with the bereaved might seem particularly valuable as part of ministering to them. Many clergy reckon that this might be a better use of their time than the pre-funeral call, although they have no evidence for such a view. But they come up against the fact that time is limited. In the light of this the minister needs to recall the context within which he is working. It is not a one-to-one relationship with the bereaved. He has been used for what he represents of larger issues and horizons, as well as for the specific role in the ritual. He is, therefore, at the early stage involved with colleagues, such as the undertaker. Later these colleagues become the bereaved members of the family and their familiar contacts. If death is regarded as an inevitable component of life, then the feed-back phase of the process will be diffuse. When people are enabled to resume responsibility for their own existence, many of them do it effectively. Bereavement is not an illness, although it may sometimes turn morbid and require counselling or medication. But for most people it proves, despite first appearances, an assimilable and often an ultimately profitable experience.

In the post-funeral phase the minister, if the bereaved remain resident in the parish, might keep an eye open for them. It is noticeable, as has already been mentioned, that if the minister works effectively at the occasional offices, he tends to meet those with whom he has been involved in a variety of settings. But the main clues to any further explicit work will be picked up in the approach phase and the ritual itself. For example, if the bereaved person seems to be alone—perhaps a widow without relatives—then it may be that the minister might make a brief call on the evening of the funeral. But if, however, friends and neighbours attend the funeral, then it is a reasonable assumption that ministry after the funeral will be carried out through neighbours exercising the natural care that small communities provide. This, however, may itself need to be assessed with care by the vicar. Figures from one survey, for example, suggest that about 37% of people found themselves without help or advice when they were bereaved.[12] If this is a local phenomenon, a church might consider a scheme of lay visitors to provide support for any who appear to need it. But even such an apparently simple and caring idea needs careful forethought. For an increasingly important characteristic within the welfare society is the development of voluntary societies for and associations of those suffering particular stress, deprivation or need. Cruse, for example, has been established for widows and their children. A number of bodies are specially concerned with infant and child death, and for the elderly such societies as Age Concern exist. These national organizations, with their local groups, are often supplemented by a neighbourhood initiative. The minister should at least be aware of what is provided.[15] In such a way he may be able to further existing, though not necessarily church-based, ministry rather than find himself, for the best of motives, in competition.

Of the occasional offices funerals can appear the least rewarding for the Christian minister. The extreme vulnerability of the bereaved makes him wary of exploiting, or seeming to exploit, them. His own personal involvement, because death is common to him (as to all), is expressed in a liturgical framework, which may seem unsatisfactory. Grim services in dingy chapels do not encourage a sense that he is about anything to do with ultimate meaning, whether in this world or the next. The amalgam of superstition associated with the hereafter, coupled with the problems of Christian belief about life after death, compound his personal questioning. Yet at the same time he feels used as a pillar of reliability and assurance in a dark moment of life. If, however, he can avoid merely colluding with expectations, either because of his own uncertainties or because of an inability to resist the seductions of people's apparent, but probably not real, needs, the minister can find in this work genuine occasion for Christian ministry. For he is being invited to stand for people where, for the moment, they feel inadequate themselves and to interpret the common human experience, death and bereavement, in the light of his supposed ability to represent God and face the unknown. Such a stance is that both of the Christian minister and, when considered carefully, of Christ himself.

Notes

1. Notably G. Gorer, *Death, Grief and Mourning in Contemporary Britain* (London, Cresset, 1965); E. Kübler-Ross, *On Death and Dying* (London, Tavistock, 1970); J. Litten, *The English Way of Death: The Common Funeral since 1450* (London, Hale, 1991).

2. J. B. McCarthy, *Death Anxiety: The Loss of the Self* (New York, Gardner, 1980).
3. J. Hick, *Death and Eternal Life* (London, Collins, 1976); P. and L. Badham, *Immortality or Extinction?* (London, Macmillan, 1982).
4. I. Ainsworth-Smith and P. Speck, *Letting Go* (London, SPCK, 1982).
5. B. A. Backer, N. Hannon and N. A. Russell, *Death and Dying: Individuals and Institutions* (New York, Wiley, 1982), especially ch. 8. Also A. Walter, *Funerals, and How to Improve Them* (London, Hodder, 1990).
6. T. G. A. Baker, '". . . and the life everlasting"?', *Theology* (1983), pp. 425ff.
7. John Donne, *Devotions*.
8. Carr, *Priestlike Task*, p. 33.
9. Reed, *Dynamics*, pp. 23ff; Carr, *Pastor as Theologian*, ch. 14.
10. In the Alternative Service Book (1980) the following sequence is offered: 1 Tim. 6.7; Job 1.21; Deut. 33.27; Lam. 3.22f; Matt. 5.4; John 3.16; Rom. 8.38f; 1 Cor. 2.9; 1 Thess. 4.14ff.
11. P. J. Hennessy, *Families, Funerals and Finances* (London, HMSO, 1980), cited in Ainsworth-Smith and Speck, *Letting Go*, p. 81.
12. See the list in Ainsworth-Smith and Speck, pp. 137ff.

PART THREE

Handling the Pressures
from the
Occasional Offices

NINE

The Minister: Pressures and Resources

Effective work at the occasional offices will absorb time and energy. Aspects of this ministry may be delegated and there are many opportunities for carefully planned collaboration between lay and ordained. Nevertheless ministry through baptisms, weddings and funerals will always rely heavily on the public minister. The unconscious dependence with which the church lives and works is such that the recognized religious figure will be deeply involved.[1] Pastors, therefore, experience this facet of their ministry as demanding. Whether in the inner city or in the countryside they are caught in a series of pressures. Not everyone will experience each of these to the same degree. But when their ministry is considered, most ministers find all or most of them to be part of their everyday experience.

This chapter offers a brief overview of these pressures, together with suggestions about some theological resources that may be overlooked. It covers in summary form areas which themselves require whole books.

Pressure from Time

Encounters through requests for the occasional offices, although brief in that they are fleeting within the total scheme of people's lives and the scale of a minister's work, take time. Diaries have to be managed, and people are not always accommodating. The competing demands for the minister's time are many and various. Ordinands are warned of the trap of busy-ness, but almost without fail ministers fall into it.[2] A practical effect of such earnestness, demonstrated by a full (often paraded) diary, is that the minister becomes less available to those who wish to approach him, while at the same time deceiving himself that he is accessible. But there is another, and more serious, consequence. That sense of reliability in the minister, which provides the link for people's felt, but unexpressed, dependence, is missing. As a result parishioners feel disabled from inviting him to work with them. It is not uncommon for those training the clergy today to find that they eagerly come to courses on counselling, but that they often end by asking how, now that they are 'trained', they can find those whom to counsel. They overlook the obvious fact that, if ministers were to do their work in the parish, they would most probably meet through the occasional offices more people than any professional counsellor and most likely would be of more use to them. The issue is not so much lack of competence in the clergy, to be remedied by training, as a blindness to their distinctive role, often induced by a false sense of the need to be busy.

Spiritual directors emphasize the need for the minister to find space and quiet so as to create these for others. Monica Furlong has written that 'the clergyman's role is to decrease his activity', and that she looks for a minister who can live in a state that is 'neither laziness nor hyperactivity'.[5] Most ministers would probably concur that such a state is desirable. But the burden of the occasional offices seems to militate against achieving it.

The question, when faced with such demand, is how brief but intense encounters can most effectively be managed. Clergy in general find difficulty in disengaging from individuals. This problem may be reinforced by any training that implies that 'intense' means 'long in time'. Time, however, as was noted earlier, is not inflexible. It changes according to perspective. If the notion of a process to be managed is given priority in considering the occasional offices, it may be that the apparent pressure of time may be seen for what it is—a question of how ministry is understood and priorities assigned.

Pressure from the Church

Ministers cannot be isolated from the assumptive world of the church of which they are members. Later we shall consider the pressures of the local church. Here the point at issue is that ecclesiastical melange of synods, councils, reports, discussions and ideas within which the local church is set. A prevailing ideology is that, if the church is to be more effective in the world, it should more clearly identify itself and draw more precisely its boundaries of belief, practice and membership. It would thus become more sure of what it has to offer and more confident in presenting it. Attention consequently is directed to the church's internal life, its organization, beliefs, liturgy, and criteria for membership. No minister can be immune from these pressures. But it can be helpful to remember that the way in which the church interacts with those who look to it for ministry has a two-way effect. Christians are accustomed to think in terms of ministry and mission as if these consisted of the church going to others with something. As a result much church time is spent trying to get the internal organization right so as to encourage these activities. But things are more complicated than that. 'Significant internal changes within a system cannot be sustained unless consistent changes occur in the relatedness of the system to its environment.'[4] This observation points to the intimate connection between the practice of ministry in specific contexts and the inner life of the church. The church's existence does not depend upon its internal correctness. Current trends, therefore, need reversing and risks once more have to be taken by engaging with people on the basis of their requests, demands and superstitions. When Christians bravely speak of losing all for the sake of the gospel, they neglect the obvious point that part of this 'all' will be those aspects of the believed gospel that they feel most inclined to preserve.

Pastors are necessarily involved in contemporary questions about how ministry is to be exercised and in major matters of church order and doctrine. But if they allow all this to be imported into their day-to-day dealings with those who turn to the church—and hence to them—for some aspect of a largely undefined ministry, they will probably be inclined to devalue the significance of those requests in order to protect themselves from the confusions of faith and practice that are being stirred up within them. To cope with such pressures, therefore, the minister will need an ordered perception of the church as she

knows and experiences it and of the task that it is per-
forming. The conclusions she reaches may be less palatable
than some of the weightier (and possibly flightier) views
of church leaders, theologians and ecumenists. But without
such an interpretative framework, she will have difficulty
in sustaining Christian ministry against pressure from
the church at large.

Pressure from the Minister

Amid the many welcome developments in thinking about
ministry today, there lurks a major hazard. Anxious for
good reason about being trapped in a false and inappropriate
professionalism, the church's ministers may encourage
the belief that they have no professional skill.[5] This may
be a gratifyingly deprecatory stance for the humble individual and an encouraging view for those lay people who
seek an alternative interest in life by acquiring office as
some sort of authorized 'minister'. But it is undermining
to any ministry by the church which may be requested
by ordinary people. When faced by intense and probably
incomprehensible feelings, such as those around the
future of a couple, a child as the embodiment of a new
era, or death as entry to the unknown, people seek focal
figures to enable them to handle them. This ministry is
more than one of personal encounter. It contributes to the
general belief systems of a society, which are significant
both for individuals and for social groupings. It is here
that the unspecific phrase 'fabric of society' becomes
appropriate.[6] As a religious figure, the minister professes
to be one in whom questions of transcendence, meaning
and God may be explored. As such he is publicly recog-
nizable as an access point to the church and hence to the
gospel. The phrase 'going into the church' as a description
of ordination is unfortunate. But it contains a practical
truth about the role of the minister in relation to the
church's task.

Sometimes ministers resist a role that is assigned to
them, because they confuse in their thinking two separable
systems in church life. There is on the one hand its public
ministry, of which they are part, which provides these
access points for people with their dependencies. On the
other hand there is the support system, by which all who

witness to the Christian faith, wherever they may be, are encouraged and enabled to be the church. As a Christian, the minister is also part of this system. If, however, he confuses the two systems by trying to delegate the occasional offices entirely to the laity, he is usually disappointed. The stress upon himself, which he is trying to reduce, is increased. He will have overlooked the nature of human expectations and in so doing will be closing down access points for the parishioners and confusing the church members. Everyone then begins to feel incompetent: those seeking the ministry through one of these offices, because they feel that they are unable to clarify their request in such a way as to get the response that they seek; the congregation because they find themselves unable to understand what these people are requesting. Another outcome is the diminishing of the role of the public minister. It is today argued that the role of the minister of religion has already been reduced. Since society is changing, this role also alters.[7] But it sometimes appears that the reduction in the role of the ordained minister owes as much, if not more, to the withdrawal of the church's ministers from this position of primary interface with the non-church people than to any greater willingness on their part to have less to do with him.

Pressure from Emotions

Every minister, however he understands the church, his role and the need for some sort of management, nevertheless comes up against the fact that ministry through the occasional offices offers limited emotional satisfaction. In spite of sudden and unexpected gratification, this ministry is more often characterized by heavy demands upon the minister's personal resources, which go unrewarded. The congregation usually expects him to do this work. Sometimes the minister may feel that contact with people around baptisms, weddings and funerals is less fraught and burdensome than dealing with yet another committee of the believing people of God. But he has in the end to face the fact that the encounters are short-lived, and that there is rarely a sense of work well done or of the people being eager to see him after he has performed his function. Sometimes strange attitudes emerge.

For example, a minister may find that the relatives of someone whose funeral he has conducted will cross the street in order to avoid him. Various ideas have been discussed throughout this book about why such eccentric behaviour occurs. But however adequately explanations may be developed and courses offered to assist ministers in appreciating human behaviour, the experience remains personally mystifying and wounding. There may be, therefore, a tendency to shrink from this type of work for unexamined emotional reasons.

Intellectually a minister may be able to ask herself why she should expect gratification. She may even be masochistically seeking to justify her feeling of hurt by means of theological or spiritual arguments. But in spite of all this, she may still, whether consciously or not, deliberately involve herself in areas of ministry which seem more warmly appreciated. In so doing she may find herself in a double bind. On the one hand, she may ask questions about the significance of Christian ministry (and ordination in particular), which she may answer in terms which release her from the public encounter with parishioners and direct her to members of the congregation or other groups in which she feels welcome. Yet the further she is involved in these worlds, the more insistent questioning of the model of Jesus' ministry with sinners, rather than with the righteous, returns to haunt her.

Pressure from Theology

As a contribution to the study of pastoral practice this book has been designed to allow the reader to raise his or her own theological questions. Here, however, after a brief consideration of the pressure upon the minister from theological issues, a transition will be made to three lines of approach, which any ministry has to take into account when dealing with human beings, and which are sometimes overlooked in theological reflections on ministry. These passages inevitably more than most draw upon the background of the Church of England. But that may be no bad thing, since the experience of this church in handling the occasional offices is, given the religious complexion of Great Britain, among the most extreme.[8]

It is a characteristic of any church that theology is

invoked by all parties to intense debate. Theological argument also needs examining for the way in which it is being used. It can be employed to avoid the work of ministry rather than to lead to it. The view taken in this book is that the church, whether it likes it or not, is still enmeshed in a series of significant ways in the lives of ordinary men and women. Any theological discussion, therefore, must include data that derive from the practice of ministry with such people. When theology is used as a means to avoid work, it is usually characterized by mention of 'principles' or 'fundamentals'. One of the principles or fundamentals, however, is that in the West the Christian church has deliberately offered itself for handling people's deepest, often irrational, emotions. Theological consequences follow from that decision, which cannot be revoked by serendipitous discovery of a so-called alternative (to some, more pristine) set of principles. The interaction of the church with its environment creates theological reflection. Perhaps too much of this interaction is today seen in terms of the individual. The church then becomes merely another facet of the individual believer's life, with which he or she alone has to interact. Such narcissism can scarcely have a future, since it is an inevitably sterile encounter with a presumed self. But one ministerial outcome is both pastoral and theological. Since individuals and their link with the church are the focal point of interpretation, the attempt is made to impose a theological framework of understanding upon people so that they can be believed by the church to be capable of receiving ministry. But in so doing theological presumptions are only confirmed and not explored. Pastoral concern for people as human beings is reduced to manipulation, rather than to discerning their intrinsic value to God and their significance for the church.[9]

Theological Indications for Ministry through the Occasional Offices

The church's self-understanding and its interpretation of God's world will be furthered as its theology is scrutinized in the light of the practice of Christian ministry. The sacraments, for example, have been seen to be both signs to the world and symbols to the church. Theological learning works in a similar way, in so far as it is informed by ideas that derive from the church's interactions with God's creation, and specifically with men and women in their everyday experience. Three useful, but often neglected, aspects of such thinking are wisdom, representation and inclusive exclusiveness.

Donald Capps has developed a theory of 'Pastoral Care as Therapeutic Wisdom' in which he brings together the Wisdom tradition and Erikson's life-cycle theory. He describes the three major disorienting experiences of life as moral confusion, inability to grasp meaning, and severe suffering. These are addressed respectively in three books of Wisdom—Proverbs, Ecclesiastes and Job.[10] From time to time the Wisdom tradition is explored in the church, but it seems to have little obvious impact on contemporary ministry. While the world looks for wise men, Christian ministers seem more enthused by the aggressive image of the prophet or the self-ridiculing likeness of the clown. Neither of these stances is discredited. Prophetic discernment is a facet of any ministry, and wise folly is one view of pastoral care.[11] But the Wisdom tradition, perhaps in not so schematized a way as in Capps' approach, has profound aspects, which are valuable reference points for thinking about pastoral ministry. The realities of life, its opportunities, injustices, hopes and fears, are its chief topic. This tradition is located where people today feel themselves to be. Occasionally it declines into cynicism—an experience which is not unknown to ministers—but its basic orientation is towards hope. It values everything, including the small and apparently insignificant things of everyday life. Theological interpretation, therefore, is based upon the simple stance of first trusting people and then offering them interpretations about transcendence and meaning. As a theological attitude the Wisdom tradition enlarges the options within what is the case, rather than limiting them through presuppositions or diminishing the impact of available evidence. To magnify God it is not necessary to devalue human life. Wisdom, therefore, is essentially a loving approach to God's world, since in so trusting mankind, God is classically presented as letting-be, which is the heart of the nature of divine love.[12]

The second model, the idea of representation, derives from Second Isaiah. In that text the notion of God's servant is amplified in a series of somewhat mysterious songs. The chief characteristic of this servant is that he can accept delegation from God to be what God wishes him to be on his behalf. To do this he does not initially have to be personally in touch with God. His vocation depends not upon his worthiness, spirituality or acceptability, but solely upon his being chosen by God as his representative. Hence, by a profound insight, the writer can even claim that the enemy of God's people can be God's anointed. Cyrus becomes the anointed prince, chosen by God to be his pastor (Isa. 24.28ff). In order to make such a claim, the prophet has to sustain certain other views: God is the only God, and people's behaviour, however inexplicable, cannot be ascribed to devotion to another; God is the creator of all things, and therefore is not preoccupied with his chosen people alone; this God is continually creating something new, in this instance a new exodus; and the suffering of God's people is, as it always has been, a vocation for the benefit of all mankind. Such themes seem vital as points of reference for any pastoral minister who can perceive that the church's focus of concern can never be those who are members of its congregations.

Thirdly, there is the question of the comprehensiveness of any theology. There is a natural tendency among religious people to affirm positions in order to exclude consideration of their converse and to make excited affirmations in order to eschew what is being denied. The history of Christian theism, for example may be seen in this perspective.[13] One particularly acute form of this for the Christian is the struggle between each person's individuality and their corporate context. In the New Testament this striving comes primarily to the fore as the writer of the Fourth Gospel consistently affirms the individual and his or her decisions by giving them without fail a corporate context and significance. So, for example, the individual is saved only in the context of the world's salvation as a whole (John 3.16); the crucifixion of the one man is also his glorification in order to draw the whole world to him (John 12.37). Christian belief is marked by a powerful exclusiveness. The believer is called out from the rest of the world. But once acknowledged, this exclusive behaviour becomes utterly, and sometimes embarrassingly, inclusive. Christians are asked to recognize a form of representation for the very people from whom they have, by an act of faith, dissociated themselves. This stance is one that the pastor has to pursue theologically for himself. For he faces it regularly in his daily encounters with individuals and the wider significance that each carries. He also requires some such approach to questions of his own personal individuality and how that is to be valued, not only for his day-to-day dealings with parishioners but for all aspects of his ministry, when this is viewed *sub specie aeternitatis.*

These three models, which have been sketchily outlined, may help pastors orient themselves towards continuing ministry in the face of those pressures which were discussed earlier. They also provide points of contact between the minister's own spiritual life of prayer and its development and his public life as a live symbol. The near cynicism of the Wisdom writers will never be far from his experience. Nor will he be unfamiliar with the extraordinary vehicles that God can use to convey a message to the community of the faithful. And, as has been consistently argued, the way in which exclusive aspects of human life and of Christian witness may become implicitly inclusive, is something with which the minister, like the writer of the Fourth Gospel, permanently struggles. In this maelstrom of experience and reflection the minister may then notice that at various times Jesus Christ is understood as the wisdom of God, the servant of God, and finally as the crucified one who draws all to himself.

Conclusion

The five pressures, however, especially when they coincide, can prove overwhelming. Understanding may help, but two further parts of ministerial preparation are required: vision and learning. The emphasis in this book has been on seeing these brief encounters as processes through which people and minister go together. It is an interpretative—essentially priestly—ministry. The vision needed for such a ministry may be of the opportunities presented in the most unlikely guises. But equally requisite is a vision which encompasses the process itself. Majesty and disaster are integral to it. The pastoral relationship introduces pastors, if only they can grasp this vision, to the 'public ills of the world as well as to the great themes of the Christian faith'.[14] To hold such a vision in touch with reality requires a commitment to the way of Christ and a firm grasp on the fact of the church, as it exists by interaction between itself and God's world. Risking exploration through these pastoral ministrations will enlarge the vision of the occasional offices as well as that of the ministry of the Christian church.

As for training, this has been mentioned from time to time in the course of the discussion. It has no magic of its own, and operates under constraints. Practising pastors have only limited time at their disposal for study in any field. And ministers need to sustain a wider perspective upon themselves and their work than is implied by specific learning about the occasional offices. They have been described in this book primarily as being aware of their role and willing to risk scrutiny and exploration of themselves as a means to serving the church's task. Mere acquisition of believed skills will not greatly assist him. The essentials are a consistent framework which gives a strong sense of role. Once this is discerned, training—or better, development—is coherently linked through the framework, and a range of approaches is evaluated in the light of it. Such training does not lead to the disowning of one's responsibilities, but to a clearer, personal grasp of what they might be and, what is more, what they might signify.

Vision and training, which themselves are not connected, may be directed to a common aim—the better understanding and performance of Christian ministry and a recovery of the clergy's pastoral function in the light of the new demands that are made upon it by the contemporary world. To that end the occasional offices, fraught as they are with various practical and theological problems, may nevertheless still be regarded as a means and not an unfortunate hindrance.

Notes

1. Carr, 'Working with dependency and keeping sane', in Ecclestone, *Parish Church?*
2. J. S. Stewart, *Heralds of God* (London, Hodder, 1946), p. 170: 'Beware the professional busy-ness which is but slackness in disguise.'
3. Monica Furlong, *New Christian* 16 June 1966, p. 12.
4. E. J. Miller, 'Open systems revisited; a proposition about development and change', in W. G. Lawrence ed., *Exploring Individual and Organisational Boundaries* (London, Wiley, 1979), pp. 217ff.
5. For approaches to professionalism see A. Russell, *The Clerical Profession* (London, SPCK, 1980) and *The Continuing Education of the Church's Ministers*, GS Misc 122 (London, CIO, 1978).
6. Habgood, *Church and Nation*, pp. 93ff.
7. S. Ranson, A. Bryman and B. Hinings, *Clergy, Ministers and Priests* (London, RKP, 1977).
8. D. Jenkins, *The British: Their Identity and Their Religion* (London, SCM, 1975), pp. 59ff.
9. Carr, *Pastor as Theologian.*
10. D. Capps, *Life-Cycle Theory and Pastoral Care* (Philadelphia, Fortress, 1983), pp. 99f.
11. On 'prophet' see Carr, *Pastor*, and on 'wise folly' see A. V. Campbell, *Rediscovering Pastoral Care* (London, DLT, 1981).
12. W. H. Vanstone, *Love's Endeavour, Love's Expense* (London, DLT, 1977).
13. J. Macquarrie, *In Search of Deity* (London, SCM, 1984).
14. Selby, *Liberating God*, p. 8.

Index

141